THE
AMULET
MANUAL

A GUIDE
TO UNDERSTANDING
AND MAKING YOUR OWN
AMULETS

First published by O Books, 2007
O Books is an imprint of John Hunt Publishing Ltd.,
The Bothy, Deershot Lodge, Park Lane, Ropley, Hants, SO24 0BE, UK
office1@o-books.net
www.o-books.net

Distribution in:

UK and Europe
Orca Book Services
orders@orcabookservices.co.uk
Tel: 01202 665432 Fax: 01202 666219 Int. code (44)

USA and Canada
NBN
custserv@nbnbooks.com
Tel: 1 800 462 6420 Fax: 1 800 338 4550

Australia and New Zealand
Brumby Books
sales@brumbybooks.com.au
Tel: 61 3 9761 5535 Fax: 61 3 9761 7095

Far East (offices in Singapore, Thailand, Hong Kong, Taiwan)
Pansing Distribution Pte Ltd
kemal@pansing.com
Tel: 65 6319 9939 Fax: 65 6462 5761

South Africa
Alternative Books
altbook@peterhyde.co.za
Tel: 021 447 5300 Fax: 021 447 1430

Text copyright Kim Farnell 2007

Design: Stuart Davies

ISBN: 978 1 84694 006 4

A CIP catalogue record for this book is available from the British Library.

Printed in the US by Maple Vail

THE
AMULET
MANUAL

A GUIDE
TO UNDERSTANDING
AND MAKING YOUR OWN
AMULETS

KIM FARNELL

BOOKS

Winchester, UK
Washington, USA

CONTENTS

INTRODUCTION TO AMULETS

Even today, we commonly make use of symbols, to denote not only objects, but also to describe events and abstract ideas. Every letter that we write is the survival of a picture, and therefore the symbol of a separate idea.

An amulet is a symbol and may be as simple as a pebble or a feather, or it may be a parchment bearing writing or other meaningful symbols. The meaning and significance that you attribute to the symbol is what is important. It can be created by yourself or someone else and works as a tool to activate our subconscious mind.

From the earliest days of prehistory, humanity has protected itself with the use of amulets, objects imbued with mysterious and magical powers. Amulets come and go in fashion over the years but their purpose endures.

The word "amulet" probably comes from the Latin word *amuletum* or the old Latin term *amoletum*, which means, "means of defense." Alternatively, the word may be derived from the Arabic *hamalet* meaning "that which is suspended."

Faith in amulets was almost universal in the ancient world. The ancient Assyrians, Egyptians, Babylonians, Arabs, and Hebrews all placed great importance in amulets.

They were used extensively in medicine, and are mentioned in ancient treatises on natural history and on the virtues of plants and stones.

In their earliest form, amulets were natural objects. Some of the ancient amulets that survive in museums today are rough, unpolished fragments of such stones as amber, agate, cornelian, and jasper. Others are wrought into the shape of beetles, quadrupeds, eyes, fingers, and other members of the body. The selection of stones, perhaps to be strung together in necklaces, was often made with reference to their reputed virtues. As civilization progressed, amulets were fashioned into symbols, seals, rings, and plaques.

An amulet is usually worn on the body, often around the neck, but some are hung up to guard homes, tombs and buildings. Amulets usually comprise a pouch or bag that contains an inscribed or otherwise powerful object.

All sorts of substances have been employed as charms, some of them seemingly odd, such as dried toads. Generally, they consist of stones, herbs, or passages written on paper. Two universal amulet symbols are eyes and phallic symbols. Eyes protect against the evil eye, and phallic symbols against evil in general.

Sometimes the amulet consists of a spoken, written, or drawn magic formula, such as *abracadabra*, a magical formula used by the Gnostics to invoke the aid of benevolent spirits to ward off disease and affliction, and the magic square, or *kamea*, a square with numbers that whether read vertically, horizontally or diagonally form the same sum.

Most cultures believe that the words of sacred religious books such as the Quran, Torah, and Bible possess protective powers. Bits of parchment containing quotes from these books are carried in pouches or boxes as amulets. Ancient pagans wore figurines of their gods as amulets. This is similar to the practices of the Catholic religion where some members still wear scapulars and medals of the saints.

In Christian art, symbolism occupies as large a place as in the pagan mythology of old. For example, a figure holding a key with sometimes a cock in the background represents St. Peter; a man in a boat typifies Noah; the fish is a symbol of Christ.

Amulets fashioned from the various names of God and magical words and numbers were particularly popular during the Renaissance to the early nineteenth century. They were used to provide protection and were accompanied by *grimoires*, books of magical instruction written for and by magicians. In magic, using the name of a deity is the same as drawing down divine power. The *Tetragrammation*, which is the Hebrew personal name for God, and translates into our alphabet as YHWH (pronounced Yahweh), is believed to be very powerful in magic operations and has been fashioned into amulets using different spellings. It is believed to help magicians in conjuring up demons and give protection from negative spirits.

Using amulets can become a prayer practice when the object connotes a communication to the divine, or is carried as a reminder of the sacred. For example, Buddhist prayer stones represent a range of spiritual figures; Islamic amulets are carved in calligraphy with scriptural verses or a list of the attributes of God; and Catholics wear medals depicting saints. Contemporary *WWJD* jewelry in the USA reminds the wearer to ask, "What would Jesus do?" in challenging circumstances. Taoists in China use amulets for healing and protection while users of amulets in Japan often have intentions that are more specific, such as scholastic success. In neo-pagan witchcraft, the most powerful amulet is the silver pentacle, the symbol of the craft. The sign of the pentacle, called a pentagram, is used to protect sacred sites.

Pliny, the Roman naturalist, described three types of amulets: those that offered general protection, those that prevented disease, and substances used as medicine. Amulets provide people with health, luck, fertility, power, success, and almost any other need. In ancient civilizations, the forces of good and evil controlled these needs. Prayers, offerings, and sacrifices were offered to the good spirits to grant blessings, while amulets stopped the evil spirits from taking them away.

Although we're not always aware of what we're doing, we all use amulets. That is, we ascribe significance to inanimate objects and find that it works. For example, wedding rings are worn to remind the wearer of their vows. Sports teams carry mascots and many people carry a lucky four-leaved clover or have a horseshoe above their door. Millions of Christians use the crucifix or cross to remind them of Christ's sacrifice. Amulets can be found in all cultures and are very popular in countries such as India and Africa.

Many people wear amulets for protection. Protection is a vague concept and although an amulet can be made to assist in general protection, its will work better if you are more specific when designing the amulet. If you are afraid of a person, an illness, or a situation, then focus your amulet on that and design it accordingly.

The words and symbols used are very important. They are drawn as links with the spiritual energies that they are intended to represent and indicate a connection with the magical energies you seek to invoke. The Hebrew alphabet is traditionally used but the Latin (as in English), Greek or Arabic alphabets can be used. Symbols impress on your mind the nature of your intent and the nature of the force or energy that the amulet represents. There are many types of symbols that can be used. Sigils are symbols used to charge amulets and impress on your mind the nature of the force or energy of your intent. Sigils can be created using magic squares (*kameas*).

An amulet can contain a talisman. Some authorities have used the term *talisman* to refer to a charm that wards off negative influences and *amulet* for a charm that serves as a magnet for good. The definitions of each term vary depending on the source.

The word *talisman* is derived from the Arabic *tilsam* "a magical image" through the plural form *tilsamen*. This Arabic word is itself probably derived from the Greek meaning "a religious mystery" or "consecrated object."

A talisman is often defined as an astrological or other symbol expressive of the influence and power of one of the planets, engraved on a sympathetic stone or metal, or inscribed on specially prepared parchment, under the auspices of that planet. Amulets and talismans with inscriptions are sometimes called charms.

In this book, we use the term *amulet* throughout. Whether charms, talismans or amulets, they are always material objects, in which no spirit resides either permanently or occasionally, but which are associated with something. They therefore become charged with the properties of the thing and may protect the owner from foes or they may be lucky.

Amulets have been found in all cultures for thousands of years. The reason that they have existed for so long is simple – they work. Amulets can be easy to make and no special equipment is needed, simply a basic knowledge of the process involved. Before we go on to look at how you can make your own amulets, let's take a short look at the rich heritage of the history of the amulet.

CHAPTER 1

THE HISTORY OF AMULETS

It's impossible to say where and when amulets where first used. Originally, they were simply natural objects. As time went on, amulets were wrought into animal shapes, symbols, seals, rings, and plaques. These were imbued with magical powers and inscribed with spells.

Amulets come in two main forms – those inscribed with magical formulae and those that aren't. When magical words are cut on the amulets, they gain the power of both the substance they're made from and the power that lies in the words themselves.

Amulets were used to protect the human body from evil baleful influences, and from the attacks of visible and invisible foes. Some amulets represent beliefs and superstitions that are so old that even the ancient Egyptians were doubtful about their origin and meaning.

Assyrians and Babylonians

Cylinder seals (cylinders engraved with pictures used in ancient times to roll an impression onto a sheet of wet clay) were used by the Assyrians and Babylonians. Precious and semi-precious stones were embedded inside the seals, each possessing their own powers. Animal-shaped amulets were common, for example, the ram for virility and the bull for virility and strength.

Egyptians

The ancient Egyptians were great users of amulets, many of which depicted Egyptian gods. The earliest known amulets from ancient Egypt (found in graves) date to about 4000 BCE. Natural items that resembled some other objects were believed to have a kind of sympathetic magic. For example, shells resembling female genitals were used to make girdles to ensure fertility. Some amulets were made of herbs, animal parts, or hair wrapped in linen and tied with a cord. Even a simple knotted cord could be an amulet.

The majority of ancient Egyptian amulets were fashioned into the form of a living creature (representing a god or goddess. The most usual was the bull's head, but other creatures were also used such as the hawk, serpent, crocodile, and the frog.

Although most amulets were worn around the neck, some Egyptian amulets were massive, such as the stone beetle mounted on a pedestal at Karnak, measuring five feet long by three feet wide and weighing more than two tons.

Gradually, animal forms began to disappear to be replaced by inscribed plaques. The earliest name for the formulae found upon amulets is *hekau*. It was so important for the deceased to be provided with these words of power, that in the sixteenth century BCE a special section was inserted in the *Book of the Dead*.

Examples of Egyptian Amulet Symbols

♡ Heart

The heart is the seat of life and the source of both good and evil thoughts. Heart amulets were often made in the form of the scarab. The scarab possesses remarkable powers. It not only protects the dead, but also gives new life to the wearer. The scarab was the symbol of the god Khepera, the invisible power of creation who propelled the sun across the sky.

Vulture

The vulture causes the power of the goddess Isis to protect the deceased and was placed on their neck on the day of their funeral

Eye of Horus

The eye of Horus amulet, or *Utchat* is a very common Egyptian amulet.

It comes in two forms, facing left and right. Together they represent the two eyes of Horus, one of which was white and the other black. One Utchat represents the Sun and the other the Moon (or Râ and Osiris). When worn, it brings strength, vigor, protection, safety, and good health.

⚤ **Ankh**

The ankh symbolizes life and is usually worn as a pendant.

⚲ **Nefer**

Nefer signifies happiness and good luck and is often worn as a pendant.

🐸 **Frog**

The frog-headed goddess Heqt is associated with resurrection.

The Arabs

Arabs, and later other Moslem cultures, used amulets to protect themselves from evil. Early amulets were often small bags containing dust from tombs or pieces of paper on which were written prayers, spells, magical names or the attributes of God.

Amulets were used on horses, camels, and donkeys as well as for people. They could be worn around the neck and as rings, anklets, and girdles. The ringing noises of metal charms were used to drive away demons.

Amulets that hang around the neck were universal in Arab pre-Islamic days and were called *tamima*. When a boy reached puberty, the *tamima* was cut off.

A popular amulet, still used today, is the *Amulet of the Seven Covenants of Solomon*. It consists of a strip of paper seventy-nine inches in length and four inches in width, with portions covered with red, yellow, green, or gold paint. It is rolled up, tied, and put into a case of leather and silver in order to be worn.

Moslem amulets commonly contain herbs, along with a piece of paper with Arabic writings (verses from the Quran) and magic squares. Moslem tradition states that Mohammed sanctioned the use of spells and magic so long as the names were only the names of God or of good angels.

Examples of Islamic Amulet Symbols

☾ The Crescent

Crescents guard against witchcraft and danger. The crescent is the origin of the Western lucky horseshoe and today is recognized as a symbol of Islam.

Hamsa

The *hamsa* protects against the evil eye. The word *hamsa* means "five," and refers to the fingers. It's also known as the Hand of Fatima, named for Mohammed's daughter. In Judaism, the same symbol is called the *hamesh* or Hand of Miriam.

The Hebrews

Hebrew amulets could consist either of an object inscribed with the name of God, accompanied by a scripture passage, or of the root of an herb. Grains of wheat wrapped in leather also sometimes served as amulets.

Furniture and household belongings were protected by inscribing the name of God on foot rests and handles. Men usually wore amulets on their arms or occasionally carried them in their hand. Women and children wore them on necklaces, rings, or other items of jewelry. An amulet would sometimes be placed in a hollow stick. It was more effective when no one suspected its presence. The Hebrews wore crescent moons to ward off the evil eye and attached bells to their garments to ward off evil spirits. Jewish amulets were often used to protect women during pregnancy and shield the newborn. In the Middle Ages, Christians employed Jews to make amulets for them. Traditionally, an amulet is supposed to have special power if it has Hebrew letters on it.

The Romans

The Romans didn't restrict the meaning of the word amulet to objects hung around the body. A bat carried around a house three times and hung head downward over the window was considered an amulet. Similarly, the gall bladder of a male black dog was used as a fumigant to protect the home from magic. However, most medical amulets were worn, usually around the neck, although many were attached to the left arm. The amulet was worn on or near the part of the body needing protection.

Medical amulets were enclosed in various kinds of containers such as golden lockets or boxes. The color of the container used was considered to be very important. Amulets called *bullas* were hung from children's necks on their birthday to protect them from the evil eye. A *bulla* was a locket that concealed the real amulet.

South American Amulets

Love amulets were common in South America and were made from stone representing two embracing figures. The magicians claimed that the amulets hadn't been cut but were formed by nature and if you wore one of the amulets, you would attract the person you desired. These special amulets were called *huacanqui* and *cuyancarumi*.

Medicine men and women often carried a quartz crystal that they claimed had been entered by a spirit who lived in one of the great volcanoes. The spirit inspired a knowledge of what should be said to those who came for advice or forecasts.

African Fetishes

A fetish is a statue or object with magical power. Many tribes believed that the fetishes gained their power through the ritualistic carving and consecration, the addition of special substances and the activation of its spirit by offering sacrifices and magic words. Some fetishes have the heads or stomachs hollowed out to hold special substance or mirrors to reflect back evil or to blind hostile spirits.

The Japanese

Omamori are Japanese amulets dedicated to Shinto deities as well as Buddhist figures. The word *mamori* means "protection" and *omamori* "honorable protector." The amulet covering is usually made from cloth and contains papers or pieces of wood with prayers written on them to bring good luck. They often describe on one side the area of luck or protection they're intended for and have the name of the shrine or temple they were bought from on the other. Omamori should never be opened or they lose their protective capabilities.

Thai Penis Amulets

The Thai name for a penis amulet is *palad khik*, meaning "honorable surrogate penis." The amulets are worn by boys and men on a waist-string under the clothes to attract and absorb any magical injury directed towards them. Some men wear several palad khiks at one time for different purposes. There isn't a female equivalent although women often wear a circular disk amulet called a *chaping*.

Palad khiks often contain Buddhist inscriptions, today written in an old form of script that cannot be read by contemporary Thais. They are carved from wood, bone, or horn by monks.

The Middle Ages

From the Middle Ages through the seventeenth century, numerous manuscripts appeared about amulets, consisting of practical guides, philosophical treatises and works that discussed their legitimacy.

Amulets designed to protect against the evil eye began to appear in the Middle Ages. Many silver, lead and pewter amulets have survived and it appears that metal was the preferred material for amulet making – although it may simply be that metal's durability means that more examples have survived.

With the advent of printing and stamping techniques, amulets were mass-produced in metal and paper as pendants, small sheets, or broadsides. Popular images appearing on amulets include the protective hand, fish, and angels. A few examples have crude pictures of the demonic forces the amulet will ward off. The crudity of the demonic illustrations is deliberate and another way of degrading the power of the evil spirits.

The science of talismans was a notable part of the Arabic learning received in Europe in the twelfth and thirteenth centuries and captured the interest of many major thinkers, including Albertus Magnus, Thomas Aquinas, and Marsilio Ficino.

Knowledge of precious stones and their use or curative purposes was widespread. For example, a Bohemian manuscript list of precious stones dated 1391 lists fifty-five different gems.

In the sixteenth century, sapphire, emerald, ruby, garnet, jacinth, coral, and sardonyx were used in tonics to protect against the effects of poison and the plague. If the amulet didn't work, it was advised that spurious stones were being used. This explanation was given either because apothecaries didn't have the knowledge to recognize genuine stones, or because they were trying to make a profit by substituting an inferior stone.

The Seventeenth Century

Around the turn of the seventeenth century a new kind of amulet literature emerged that treated amulets as evidence of ancient civilizations. Antiquarians viewed amulets as material objects laden with meaning to be decoded by placing them in context. This new type of amulet literature was usually illustrated, but the images were different from those in medieval literature. Traditional treatises gave the designs to be placed on amulets, but antiquarian amulet literature presented representations of specific artifacts.

Treating amulets as evidence of the beliefs and practices of past civilizations didn't require anyone to disbelieve in them. However, reading an amulet as a record of the past tended to disenchant it.

It might seem that amulets have waned in popularity in the modern world, but it's still common for Westerners to carry a rabbit's foot, covet a four-leaved clover and attach a horseshoe over their door. Many Moslems still carry containers that hold religious texts. Mascots are adopted for sports teams and many people have lucky items of clothing, brought out for certain occasions. The use of amulets is as popular now as it ever has been.

CHAPTER 2

MAKING YOUR AMULET

We can draw on traditional knowledge and the symbols used in the past to make our own amulets. Some things never change. People today seek help in love as they did thousands of years ago. Many would appreciate some form of protection from what the world throws at us, and few people would turn down something that could help them finanically.

This book provides a guide to how you can make your own amulet. An amulet has a purpose. All aspects of its design and creation are oriented towards a particular goal. It's assembled and constructed within the context of ritual and usually a blessing or consecration towards its purpose is given.

An amulet is a type of spell that has been cast as a solid object. It can be as simple or as complex as you wish and any shape or size you desire. Usually, amulets are made to protect, to attract, or to dispel specific forces and energies. The solidity of an amulet gives you something concrete to focus on and reminds you of what you're trying to achieve.

The Purpose of Your Amulet
The first step in creating your own amulet is to decide what its purpose is. You may want to create an amulet for protection, or to draw love to you. The purpose of your amulet will, to an extent, dictate the materials you use and the way that you construct it. Once you have decided the form that your amulet is going to take, you can work out the appropriate colors, materials, images, and so on that you want to use. These can be mixed and matched until you find a combination that is pleasing to you. In later chapters, there are detailed accounts of the associations of herbs, colors, and materials that will help you to choose something suitable. Here we are simply looking at the basic principles.

It can be very tempting to use everything you come across that seems relevant to your amulet. This could make it extremely complicated, time consuming to make, and potentially expensive. Keeping it simple is the best approach. Use what you think will most powerfully represent your purpose.

So that you're clear about the purpose of your amulet, it's best to write it down on a piece of paper. Some people choose to actually write or inscribe this purpose on the amulet itself. It isn't necessary to do this. However, there's no wrong way to design an amulet or talisman, or to conduct the ritual to consecrate it. As long as you know what each symbol you use means, and you imbue it with your will to achieve that purpose, it will be effective.

You can make an amulet for any purpose, though they are most commonly used for things like stimulating creativity, increasing prosperity, improving communication, drawing success, and overcoming problems.

Materials

Amulets can be made out of parchment, metals, skin, paper, oils, wood... anything at all. Metal holds forces well and lasts. Paper may be better for something temporary. The type of material you choose will depend on a variety of factors; the amount of money you wish to spend, any skills you have working with certain materials, the aesthetic value of materials, and the traditional associations of materials. A very simple amulet can be drawn on a piece of paper and worn or carried. The paper can be put with a complementary stone in a small bag for a more complex amulet. You might also add a complementary herb or other items.

Metals

If you are going to use metals as a base, make sure that you use the appropriate metal. If you are skilled in working with metal, then you can make and inscribe the amulet yourself, once you have decided on a design. Or you may choose to design the amulet and pay someone to inscribe it for you. A simple way of using metals is to simply incorporate a chip of the appropriate metal in your design.

Parchment or Paper

The oldest type of amulet is the parchment amulet. Few of these survive, due to their fragile nature. After being written, a parchment amulet might be hung on the wall or, more commonly, placed in a metal case and worn around the neck. Parchment amulets tend to be more elaborate than their metal counterparts, since the writing surface is larger and easier to work on. Parchment is preferable to paper, and you should choose the best quality you can obtain. The writing and drawing on the parchment should be in ink that's an appropriate color for your purpose. If you're using paper, you can choose paper of a suitable color. Alternatively, you can use a solution of food dye or ink and soak your parchment or paper in it to ensure that it's the appropriate color before drawing your design. Parchment or paper amulets are the cheapest and easiest to make when you're beginning. When placing parchment or paper into an amulet bag, you may want to wrap it in plastic wrap first to keep it waterproof .

Herbs

Herbal amulets are made up from combinations of herbs, written wishes and any other natural object gathered into an appropriately colored bag. Herbal amulets are also called medicine bags, power bags, mojo bags, and sachet bags in different cultures. Gather the herbs you wish to use along with a bag. The bag should be made of a natural fiber like cotton or silk. Place a pinch of each herb in the bottom of the bag, along with anything else you wish to include, for example a paper or parchment amulet. As you place each herb in the bag focus on the properties of the herb. Tighten the strings of the bag and leave it overnight to soak up and blend the energies.

If you are making a sachet-type herbal amulet, place a four-inch square piece of cloth flat on your table. Concentrating on the properties of each herb, place a pinch in the center of the material. Taking two opposite corners of the material, gently draw them up and together, and then do the same with the other corners. Twist gently but tightly and then tie with a ribbon or string made of the appropriate color.

You can wear your herbal amulet, keep it in your pocket or purse, store it in the glove box of your car, or keep it in an area where you want it to have an influence. For example, you can keep a prosperity amulet in your wallet or sleep with an amulet under your pillow.

Gemstones

Appropriate gemstones can be carried in your pocked or in a small bag. Alternatively, you can have a stone set in jewelry. If you are skilled in making jewelry, you can choose stones appropriate to your purpose and wear them as necklaces or in other forms. The stone can be augmented by an appropriate symbol, representing your purpose. This can be painted or inscribed onto the stone itself, form another part of the piece if the stone is to be set in jewelry, or be on the container you use for your amulet. It isn't necessary to buy expensive and large stones. There are cheaper alternatives to expensive gems. Stones that you pick up from the ground are perfectly suitable. Anything that is appealing to you, and is an appropriate color, can be used in the same way as a gem.

Amulet Bags

Although you can simply buy a small bag for your amulet, it isn't very difficult to make one. Your amulet bag can be a work of art or very simple. It depends on what skills you have. Amulet bags are often beaded. You can sew beads onto a simple bag, forming a symbol related to your amulet.

Anything can be used to make a bag, although natural materials are best. Squares of cotton or silk, in an appropriate color, are most often used. However, it's possible to use the toe of an old pair of stockings or a thin sock if you're in a hurry. You can simply tie it with a piece of cord or ribbon in an appropriate color.

The sewing involved in making an amulet bag is minimal, and only requires a needle and thread. If you want to make a drawstring bag, cut a piece of cloth two to three inches wide by seven to ten inches long. You also need a piece of cord for the drawstring about ten inches long.

Fold down about three quarters of an inch at the top and bottom ends to hold the drawstring. Stitch straight across at both ends. Fold the cloth in half with the right sides together. Stitch along the sides of the bag, stopping at the stitching line for the drawstring pocket and allowing about a half-inch seam allowance. Turn the bag right side out. Thread the cord through and knot the ends of the cord.

Alternatively, you can make a sealed sachet. To do this cut two three-inch squares out of cloth. Place the right sides together. Stitch around the edges and leave an opening of about one inch so you can turn and fill the sachet. When you finish stitching, turn the sachet right side out. You might need to use a pencil to get the corners sharp. Insert the pencil through the opening and poke into the corners to turn them completely right side out. It is a good idea to iron the bag at this point, to make the edges straight. Fill the sachet with your chosen filling, without overfilling it. Align the two unsewn edges and stitch the opening closed.

A simple sachet can be made by taking a piece of cloth four inches square and placing a pinch of your chosen herb in its center. Take two opposite corners of the material, draw them up together, then do the same with the other corners. Twist tightly and then tie the bag with a ribbon or string in an appropriate color.

A scrap of leather can also be used. Cut a circle of about six or eight inches in diameter. Around the perimeter of the circle, piece a series of holes with a leather punch or even a simple paper punch. A cord can then be threaded through the holes, creating a small drawstring bag. Once you have made your bag you can put into it suitable herbs, small gemstones and paper sigils, images or words.

A cheap and easy container is a matchbox. You can cover the matchbox with glued-on silk, paint it or cover it with clay. Once you have a clean surface of an appropriate color, it can be decorated with suitable symbols and filled in the same way as a bag. You can add a cord if you wish to wear it around your neck.

A small metal container can also be used. In fact, any sort of container that is small enough will perform the purpose. Once an amulet is sealed, it shouldn't be opened again. When your goal has been accomplished, you can return the amulet to the universe. It can be buried or burnt and the ashes scattered somewhere that has meaning for you.

Designing Your Amulet

Once you've decided on the materials you're going to use, gather them together. It's possible that your ideas may change slightly as you work on your design. Having your materials to hand will help you to make a more practical design.

Take a piece of paper of a color that reflects the purpose of your amulet, or choose a pen of that color to write on a sheet of white paper. A traditional amulet has two sides. One side has the magic square associated with the planet that corresponds to your purpose, while the other side contains the characters and seals of the planet. An amulet may contain any images or materials that relate to your purpose. You may wish to experiment with a few designs before you find one that appeals to you.

Amulets are often circular. Therefore, you may need a compass or stencil to help you to draw your design. The circle is a most powerful magical symbol, representing the powers of the infinite. However, you can use another meaningful shape. For example, a love amulet can be constructed in the shape of a heart.

Draw your symbols slowly and imagine energy being drawn into your image. This helps to charge the talisman as you are drawing it.

When to Make Your Amulet

To maximize the power of your amulet, you should make it at a time appropriate to your purpose. For example, a love amulet should be made on a Friday or Monday. There are also appropriate hours of the day that you should use. If you want to build or acquire something new, you should make your amulet during the waxing Moon; if it is for banishing or eliminating a certain condition, the waning Moon is preferable. To help you choose the correct time, refer to Chapter 11. As it may take you several hours or days – if not longer – to complete making your amulet, the time you choose should be for when it is finished and you finally charge it. There is no need to rush; if you cut a few corners to complete the job more quickly, your amulet may still work, but it might be less effective.

Cleansing the Materials

Once you've designed your amulet and have found yourself a quiet, clean room to make it in, it's a good idea to cleanse the materials you plan to use. To do this, you can simply light candles and incense and visualize a sphere of golden-white light around your room.

If you're working with metal, you can cleanse with the four elements. First, put the metal in a dish with sand, or earth, for a day. As you do this, visualize that any impurity that pertains to earth element will be absorbed by the earth or sand in the dish. Discard the sand or earth once you've taken the metal out of it. Next, put the metal in water for one day. Proceed the same way as with earth. Next, heat the metal over a candle flame and, finally, cool the metal by swinging it through the air in circles.

If you're using paper or parchment, you need to proceed in a different way. First light a candle and some incense. A stick of frankincense is excellent. Have a cup with water and a dish with earth nearby. After meditating briefly, look at the paper and imagine it connected with the four elements, which are symbolized by the objects on your table. Imagine that the impurities are drawn away. Finally, take the paper and blow on it, imagining that all impurities are blown out of it into their respective elements. For the first blow, connect with the fire element. Next connect with the air element, then with water, and finally with earth.

You can use similar procedures with crystals and gemstones. These may also be put into salt water for a day or so. Salt is a universal cleanser that absorbs impurities and represents the fire element. You can also use salt for metal and paper.

Charging and Consecrating Your Amulet

After the amulet is complete, you can perform a ritual to consecrate it. Purify the tamulet with earth, air, fire, and water in the same way as you cleansed the materials above. Charge it with the desired effect. This may be as a chant or a prayer, or as a ritual in the form of burning a slip of paper with the purpose of the amulet written on it, and then smearing the amulet with the resulting ash. Use whichever method you're most comfortable with.

An amulet can be consecrated in numerous ways. How you choose to do it depends on your own belief system and the time you have available. Some methods are extremely complex and detailed, whereas others are straightforward and more speedy. But the basic principles remain the same whichever method you use.

The best time to consecrate your amulet is when it is complete. Therefore, you should begin by choosing a time suitable for the purpose of your amulet as described later in Chapter 8. At the least, it's a good idea to choose a time when the Moon is waxing – going from new to full – as that allows the amulet to increase in power.

If you want to spend more time consecrating your amulet, you can use the following process. Clean and tidy a place where you can perform your consecration. You don't want any distractions and should preferably dress in clean clothing. It's best to wear indoor sandals, or slippers that have not been worn outside, or to go barefoot. You may also want to take a bath or shower beforehand. Washing yourself prepares you psychologically.

Be clear about the intent of your amulet. State its purpose aloud and call upon the power you believe in. Many people chant to attune themselves with the energies they wish to access. Moslems chant the ninety-nine names of Allah and verses of the Quran, Christians recite the Psalms of David. Other beliefs have different traditions. You can write a chant in advance that expresses your own beliefs. Whatever you chose should be chanted several times, usually repeated in a cycle of ten or a hundred.

As you chant, take a deep breath and visualize a charge of bluish-white light above your head issuing a stream of energy into your head. Then exhale, breathing on the amulet, visualizing light flowing with your breath into the amulet. Imagine the images and inscriptions on it glowing and pulsating with spiritual activity and taking on a three-dimensional quality. Then continue with your chanting and repeat the process until you have completed the cycle.

To program a specific purpose into your amulet, place the palms of your hands over your amulet, visualizing the flowing energies building up in the amulet. Breathe in as you visualize energy entering you as you did previously. Then, as you breathe out, imagine that the power is flowing through your hands and palms and into the amulet. Repeat this several times until you feel the power growing beneath your palms and around the amulet. The next step is to visualize your purpose enacting itself in the energy formed around the amulet. For example, for a love amulet, imagine the object of your affections gazing lovingly at you.

Now you can affirm your intent. This is where you affirm that the process has been carried out and it is accomplished. You simply state its purpose aloud as you did previously.

At this stage, you can now anoint the amulet if you wish. First run it through incense smoke – gahru wood is the usual choice. Then anoint the four corners of the amulet with consecrated oil, starting at the upper right-hand corner and working clockwise. Use oil most suitable for your intent, or you can use misik oil for most purposes. (This is available from specialist suppliers, many of which can be found on the internet.)

You now need to seal the forces in the amulet with a symbolical gesture to sever your link with it. This is important if you're making the amulet for someone else. Various gestures of sealing can be used, for instance, the cross, pentagram, yin-yang symbol, the word Allah in Arabic, and so on. These symbols signal to your subconscious mind that the consecration has been accomplished, that the forces are to remain therein, and that no further connection is necessary. A gesture of severance further reinforces this.

With the extended index and middle finger of the right hand, trace a sign – a cross, pentagram or similar, depending on your own belief system – over the amulet. Visualize a white light emanating from your fingers and forming the symbol. This locks the forces within the amulet. Imagine that a thread exists between you and the amulet, then wave your right hand across the thread and imagine it snapping.

You can now place the amulet in any container that you've made for it, and offer thanks to any intelligences invoked during the rite and bid them to return to their natural habitat. State that you charge the amulet in the name of whichever higher power you believe in – by the virtues of the Sun, Moon, and stars and by the elemental powers of earth, air, fire, and water. Declare aloud your amulet to be empowered with the energies that you have invoked.

A simpler, and less involved way of charging your amulet is to project energy into the lines and letters on the amulet, following the outlines, one by one. You can use a pen and point it at the lines and letters as you charge. Imagine energy flowing through your hand into the pen and into the lines and letters. Imagine energy building up in the amulet. At intervals, hold the amulet two or three inches in front of your forehead. You may notice a tingling feeling, which gets stronger as the amulet is charged. Don't worry if you don't get this feeling. Just keep charging until you feel good about the charge.

CHAPTER 3

HERBAL AMULETS

Amulets may be among the oldest forms of herbal magic. Traditionally, the village wise man or woman would place a plant in a pocket or container for someone to carry about. However, their very nature means that they have not survived, so we don't know a lot about their use.

Herbal amulets are combinations of herbs, resins and essential oils, along with special stones, written wishes and any other natural object (for example a shell, acorn or feather), gathered into a bag.

You can wear the amulet, keep it in your pocket, or store it in an area where it is meant to influence. For example, you may want to keep a prosperity amulet in your wallet.

Herbs have been used in this way for thousands of years. Traditionally, herbs were thought to have innate powers of their own without further preparation. Much of their meaning is derived from their associations with the planets. The planetary energies are thought to show the effects and disposition of each plant. For example, herbs that affect the heart, ruled by the Sun, are often golden in color, thrive in sunny areas, and promote a sense of well-being and success. Older astrology texts offer long lists of plants that are associated with each of the planets. However, knowing the nature of each planet means that it's usually possible to work out for yourself which planet's energy should be associated with which herb.

Usually, herbs will be blended for optimum effect. For example, if you were making an amulet to find the perfect job, you would need to look at a combination of herbs for success, eloquence, and expansion – in other words, a combination of herbs ruled by Sun, Mercury, and Jupiter.

Although you can simply buy the herbs you want to use for your amulet, the optimum effect will be obtained if you can collect them at a favorable astrological time. If you have astrological knowledge – or access to a friendly astrologer – you can choose a time when the planet that rules your chosen herb is in a position of strength. However, you can still successfully create an herbal amulet without going through this stage, as even with astrological knowledge, the herbs you choose to use may not grow in a location that is accessible to you. Each planet rules a huge variety of herbs and plants, so if one isn't easily obtained it should be simple to find another one to use for the same purpose. Herbs ruled by the same planet do differ slightly, so it helps when making your choice to consider the appearance of the plant, whether you're using its leaves, fruit or roots, and where it grows naturally.

There sometimes appears to be a wide variance in the list of herbs and plants associated with a specific planet. This is because the different parts of the plant have different rulerships and uses. For example, roots are thought to influence the brain, stems the skeletal structure, and flowers the lower belly and genitals. Whichever planet rules it, a plant that bears fruit is related to Jupiter, its flowers relate to Venus, seed or bark to Mercury, wood to Mars, Saturn to roots, and leaves to the Moon. As well as the planet that traditionally rules the plant, it can be thought of as having a secondary ruler according to the part of the plant being used.

Most of the rulerships now used survive from lists written in the seventeenth century, and these lists were often simplified from earlier sources. In modern textbooks, you often find lists that have been simplified even further by associating plants with zodiac signs instead of with planets.

Although you don't need to work with a highly complex system of establishing which herb will be suitable for your purposes, you can make your amulet more powerful by paying attention to some of the nuances outlined above. People who use herbs in this way still commonly refer to *Culpeper's Herbal* – originally called *The English Physician*. Although this is widely available (copies can be downloaded from the internet for free), some modern versions don't contain all of the planetary associations, so if you want to study this subject, you need to make sure that you acquire a full version.

To make life easier when it comes to choosing your herbs, lists appear below. The first list consists of herbs that are associated with each of the planets, and is most useful for those of you who either know astrology, or want to learn enough astrology to incorporate it in making your amulets.

The second list gives a list of some of the herbs that can be used for making amulets for specific purposes. You may want to refer to both lists to find the optimum combination of herbs for the amulet you have in mind.

Planets and Herbs

Sun

These herbs promote self-confidence and personal success. They impart a sense of purpose and help develop a sense of identity and willpower. Sun herbs bring vitality, health, creativity, and dignity. They are plants that smell pleasant, grow majestically, and love the Sun and are usually red or yellow.

Angelica, ash, barley, bay, calendula, cedar, celandine, chamomile cinnamon, dittany, frankincense, ginger, heliotrope, ivy, lavender, lovage, marigold, marjoram, orange and lemon tree peony, pepper, rosemary, rue, saffron, sundew, sunflower, vervine, St. Johns wort, walnut, vine.

Moon

These herbs affect the subconscious mind. They aid in the development of intuition. They include all herbs that turn towards the Moon. All Moon trees and plants are juicy and full of sap. The herbs have leaves that are thick, round, soft and juicy. The plants also include those without much flavor, such as unripe fruits. Moon herbs are often white or pale in color.

Adders tongue, cabbage, columbines, cucumber, endive, honesty, ivy, jasmine flowers, lettuce, lily, linseed, melon, mugwort, mushroom, palm tree, poppy, privet, pumpkin, purslane, rosemary, white sandalwood, seaweed, wallflower, watercress, white rose, willow.

Mercury

These herbs facilitate clear thinking and eloquent communication. They help in business success, where a clear head is needed, and in recovery from illness. Mercury herbs enable you to communicate more and improve your learning skills. They tend to stimulate the central nervous system and brain. They are often of mixed colors.

Cardamom, carrots, caraway, cinnamon, dill, fern, fennel, five leaved grass, hazel, honeysuckle, lavender, liquorice, marjoram, maidenhair, mastic, mulberry, oats, parsley, valerian, walnut.

Venus

These herbs bring joy, beauty, artistry, sensitivity, and compassion. Venus herbs activate love. They include all scented herbs and plants that smell pleasant and sweet. All fragrant and sweet spices belong to Venus too.

Alder, apricot, almond tree, apple tree, beans, birch, burdock, catnip, cherry, chickweed, coltsfoot, columbine cypress, cowslip, daffodil, daisy, elder, featherfew, fig tree lily, foxglove, grape, groundsel, mallow, mint, mugwort, parsnip, pear tree, peach, pennyroyal, plum, pomegranate, primrose, raspberry, rose, sorrel, strawberry, tansy, thyme, violet, valerian, vervain, vine, violet, walnut, wheat, yarrow.

Mars

These herbs give energy. They promote independence and assertiveness and stimulate the passions. Mars herbs can be used for protection and to develop or maintain motivation. When mixed with herbs of other planets they lend their energies to make the whole stronger. They include all herbs that have sharp pointed leaves and are red. Mars plants usually grow in dry places and in barren and hard, stony ground. The trees are thorny or prickly. Herbs that are red in color and burn are Mars plants.

Basil, bramble, bryony, broom, cuckoopint, flax, garlic, ginger, hawthorn, hops, mustard, nettles, onion, pepper, radish, rhubarb, thistle, tobacco, sandalwood, wormwood.

Jupiter

These herbs expand consciousness and opportunity. They bring growth on all levels and are helpful in health matters as they expand the body's ability to heal itself. They expand the mind allowing for a greater understanding. Herbs and plants of Jupiter tend to be large.

Agrimony, almond, asparagus, ash, basil, bay, birch, borage, cherry, cloves, daisy, dandelion, dock, endive, fig, gooseberry, hazel, hyssop, ivy, liquorice, mace, magnolia, marjoram, mint, mulberry, nutmeg, oak, olive, pear, peony, pine, pomegranates, red rose, rhubarb, saffron, sage, St. Johns wort, strawberries, sugar, wheat, violets, vine.

Saturn

These herbs give structure, foundation, grounding, and stability. They teach that success comes through perseverance and patience. Saturn herbs are binding herbs and protect in a non-aggressive manner.

Angelica, barley, beech, bindweed, box, burdock, capers, comfrey, cumin, cypress, elm, fern, fumitory, hemlock, hemp, mandrake, moss, myrrh, nightshade, orange, parsnip, patchouli, pine, poplar, poppy, pulse, rue, sage, shepherds purse, spinach, willow, wormwood, yew.

Traditionally, only the seven classical planets were used in this way. However, in modern astrology, some associations have been made between herbs and plants, and the outer planets.

Neptune

These are herbs of the mystic and useful in dream working, trance, and hypnosis. They intensify the imagination and lead to concepts, visions, and ideas. Neptune herbs can be useful for developing telepathy and astral projection. Some Neptune herbs are orange blossoms, poppies, lobelia, peach, and lotus.

Uranus

These herbs excite, energize, and stimulate. They lend themselves to inspiration, practical idealism, genius, and the development of telekinesis. They bring change and sometimes unforeseen results. Some herbs of Uranus are allspice, calamus, betel, guarana, and ephedra.

Pluto

These herbs transform and illuminate the shadow side of ourselves. They can bring about the dramatic and traumatic, and can promote growth and insight. Pluto herbs help in cases of sexually impotency. Some Pluto herbs are yohimbe, saw palmetto, damiana, rye, and amaranth.

Commonly Used Herbs and Their Uses

Amaranth	Its name comes from the Greek meaning "unwithering" and it represents immortality.
Anemone	Used against diseases.
Angelica	As an herb of the Sun, it is best gathered when the Sun or Jupiter is in Leo. Legend says that it was given to a monk by an angel to help protect humanity from the plague.
Ash Tree	Was regarded as the tree of life and used as a symbol of strength. It is used as an amulet against witches, demons, and lightening, and its leaf is an amulet for good luck. The ash is also a symbol of love as legend has it that the first bow made by Cupid was of ash.

Aster	A flower of Venus used for love amulets.
Balm of Gilead	Used to mend broken hearts.
Basil	Highly potent and used for conception.
Celedine	Prevents imprisonment.
Cinquefoile	A five-leaved herb ruled by Mercury that brings eloquence and obtains favor.
Crocus	Strengthens the heart and excites romantic impulses.
Cyclamen	A love plant that can be grown in the bedroom for protection.
Dill	Counteracts spells.
Elder	It has long been associated with death. Traditionally, a twig of elder protects against epilepsy.
Endive	Makes the wearer seem to possess all the good qualities a lover could desire.
Eyebright	Protects against eye diseases.
Frankincense	A symbol of priesthood.
Garlic	Sailors believed it protected their ships from wreckage. It can be hung from doors and windows to protect from the evil eye.
Henbane	Helps a man secure the love of a woman.
Houseleek	Used to be known as thunder flower and it was believed in the Middle Ages that it protected from lightening.

Lavender	A preserver of chastity and worn strewn in clothing.
Lotus	Revered as a sacred blossom in the East, it protects against the evil eye and brings success and luck.
Maiden Hair	Brings grace and beauty.
Mandrake	The root is a powerful aphrodisiac and can be placed under a pillow to alleviate unrequited love.
Marjoram	Used against witchcraft and to cure a cold.
Mistletoe	All-healer and should be cut on the day of a new Moon.
Moonwort	Used in love potions or to find enduring love.
Mugwort	Prevents weakness and fatigue. Used to soothe the mind and increase fertility.
Mullein	Guards against witchcraft and sorcery. When placed under a pillow it prevents nightmares.
Myrrh	Heals emotions and physical ills.
Myrtle	Used to preserve youth and love.
Oak	Jupiter's tree and a bringer of good luck
Peony	Hung round the neck it guards against storms and nightmares
Periwinkle	When hung over the door it prevents a witch from entering.
Purslane	Protects from evil spirits and when strewn beneath the bed ensures a happy home.

St. John's wort	Called the "blessed plant" it can be placed over doors and windows to keep away devils and witches.
Rosemary	A strengthener of the heart and memory, and signifies loyalty, devotion, and love.
Thyme	Protects against melancholy.
Vervain	Worn around the neck, it protects against bedwetting and makes a baby happy. It also gives soldiers escape from enemies and can reconcile enemies.

Amulet Types and Herbs

Alertness	Black pepper
Anti-theft	Caraway, garlic, juniper, larch
Aphrodisiac	Gladioli, mandrake
Beauty	Flax, ginseng, golden seal, maidenhair
Breaking love spells	Lily, pistachio
Calling spirits	Wormwood
Chastity	Cactus, camphor, coconut, cucumber, fleabane, hawthorn, lavender, lettuce, pineapple, sweet pea, vervain, witch hazel
Children	Angelica
Conception	Basil
Confusion or disruption of others	Mustard seed, poppy seed
Control	Liquorice root, poppy seeds, rosemary

Courage	Black cohosh, borage, camphor, columbine, cyclamen, elder, fennel, fern, feverfew, flax, fleabane, foxglove, frankincense, garlic, geranium, ginseng, gorse, grass, hawthorn, hazel, heather, holly, honeysuckle, hyacinth, hyssop, iris, Irish moss, ivy, juniper, lady's slipper, larch, larkspur, lavender, leek, lettuce, lilac, lily, lime, linden, liverwort, lotus, mallow, mandrake, marigold, marjoram, rue, sweet pea, ragweed, tea, thyme
Creativity	Acorns, beech, lily, mistletoe
Dexterity	Five finger grass
Divination	Goldenrod, hibiscus, ivy, lettuce, orange, pansy, pomegranate, rose, St. John's wort, willow
Dream Magic	Holly
Drive away	Eucalyptus, marjoram, oregano, pepper
Eloquence	Aspen, cinquefoile, deer's tongue
Empowering	Lemon grass leaves
Ending relationships	Turnip
Escape	Celandine
Evil spirits	Purlsane
Fatigue	Mugwort
Favors	Chicory
Fertility	Acorn, agaric, banana, barley, brackenfern, carrot, chickweed, cuckoo flower, cucumber,

cyclamen, daffodil, dock, fig,
geranium, grape, hawthorn, hazel,
horsetail, mandrake, mistletoe,
mustard, mugwort, myrtle, oak,
olive, peach, pine, pomegranate,
poppy, sunflower, wheat

Fidelity	Caraway, chili pepper, cumin seeds, coriander seeds, elder, hawthorn, liquorice, magnolia, periwinkle, raspberry leaves, rosemary, rhubarb, rye, spikenard, vervain
Fishing magic	Hawthorn
Friendship	Alfalfa, cloves, lemon, passion flower, sweet pea, yarrow
Gambling	Calendula flowers, chamomile flowers, comfrey leaf, five finger grass, Irish moss, nutmeg
Garden magic	Garlic, ginseng, grape, hibiscus, lemongrass, liquorice
Gossip or slander	Clove
Halt gossip	Slippery elm
Happiness	Catnip, celandine, chamomile, cyclamen, hawthorn, hyacinth, lavender, lily of the valley, marjoram, meadowsweet, motherwort, purslane, saffron, St. John's wort, savory, thistle, vervain
Harmony	Dulse
Healing	Althaea leaves, angelica, barley, bracken, bay, pine, caraway seed

	(protect from illness and harm), carnation, cedar, cinnamon, cypress, coriander, cowslip, cucumber, cypress, dock, elder, fennel, flax, gardenia, garlic, ginseng, groundsel, heliotrope, hemp, henna, hops, horse chestnut, ivy, liquorice, lime, myrrh, nettle, oak, olive, onion, peppermint, persimmon, plantain, plum, potato, rose, rosemary, rowan, rue, saffron, sandalwood, spearmint, thistle, thyme, tobacco, vervain, violet, willow, wintergreen
Health	Adder's tongue, blackberry, burdock, Camphor, caraway, carob, coriander, fern, geranium, groundsel, juniper, larkspur, liquorice, mandrake, marjoram, myrrh, oak, pimpernel, pine, rue, sassafras, St. John's wort, sun flower, tansy, thyme
Health and longevity	Acorn, carnation, cinquefoil, cowslip, cypress, eucalyptus, feverfew, figwort, garlic, ginseng, horse chestnut, lavender, mint, mistletoe, mugwort, myrtle, nutmeg, peach, peony, pine cones, rosemary, rowan, rue, sage, St. John's wort, spikenard, tansy, thyme, vervain, walnut, wood sorrel

Hex breaking	Wintergreen
Home and family	Althaea leaves (benevolent spirits), basil, cloves, cumin seeds, hyssop (cleansing), marjoram (protects), pennyroyal (peace)
Hunting	Yellow evening primrose
Immortality/longevity	Cypress, lavender, lemon, linden, liquorice, maple, peach, sage, tansy
Imprisonment (prevents)	Celandine
Infertility	Walnut
Joy	Orange
Legal matters	Celandine, calendula flowers, dill seed, hickory, marigold, oregano
Love	Acacia, apple blossom, apple, apricot, ash, aster, avocado, balm, barley, basil, bay, belladonna, betony, black cohosh, brazil nut, capers, cardamom seed (induce lust, passion and love), catnip (win heart), cedar, cherry, chestnut, chickweed, cinnamon, clove, clover, coltsfoot, columbine, coriander seeds, crocus, cubeb berries (control lover), cyclamen, daffodil, daisy, dandelion, dill leaf (crossed love), dogbane, elm, endive, fig, flax, fumitory, gardenia, gentian, geranium, ginger, ginseng, hemp, henbane, hibiscus, honesty, honeysuckle,

hyacinth, jasmine, juniper, lavender,
leek, lemon, lemon verbena, lettuce,
licorice, lime, linden, liverwort,
lovage, magnolia, maidenhair,
mandrake, maple, marjoram,
meadowsweet, mimosa, orange,
orchid, pansy, parsley, patchouli, pea,
peach, pear, peppermint, periwinkle,
pimento, poppy, primrose, purslane,
quince, raspberry, rose, rosemary, rue,
rye, saffron, sarsaparilla, spearmint,
spikenard, St. John's wort, strawberry,
sugar cane, tamarind, thyme, valerian,
vanilla, vervain, violet, willow,
wormwood, yarrow

Love, lost and returned	Star anise
Lover return	Daisy
Lover, new	Violet leaf
Loyalty and devotion	Rosemary
Luck	Allspice, aloe, avocado, bluebell, cabbage, caper, cinnamon, cloves, corn, daffodil, daisy, fern, frankincense, hazel, heather, holly, Irish moss, ivy, linden, lotus, meadow rue, nutmeg, oak, olive, orange, persimmon, pineapple, pomegranate, poppy seeds, poppy, purslane, rose, rowan, snakeroot, spikenard, star anise, straw, strawberry, vetivert, violet with lavender
Lust	Acorn, caper, caraway, cardamom,

	carrot, cinnamon, cyclamen, daisy, dulse, endive, ginseng, juniper berries, mastic, mugwort, nettle, olive, onion, patchouli, pear, periwinkle, radish, rosemary, saffron, sesame, sugar cane, vanilla, violet
Marriage	Clover flowers, cubeb berries, magnolia leaves, pennyroyal
Meditation	Hemp
Melancholy	Thyme
Mental powers	Grape, lily of the valley, mace, mustard, periwinkle, rosemary, rue, spearmint, vanilla, walnut
Money	Acacia, alfalfa, allspice, basil, bay, blackberry, bryony, buckwheat, cashew, cedar, cinnamon, clove, clover flowers (red), comfrey leaf, dock, hops, Irish moss, jasmine, myrtle, oak, oats, onion, orange, pea, periwinkle, pine, pineapple, poplar, poppy, sarsaparilla, sassafras, thyme, vervain, wheat.
Nightmares	Peony
Peace	Bergamot, celery seeds, chamomile, gardenia, lavender, marjoram, meadowsweet, myrtle, olive, passion flower, pennyroyal, vervain, violet.
Potency	Black cohosh, caper, oak, olive
Power	Acacia leaf, angelica root, black cohosh root, cedar, cinnamon,

cinquefoil, gentian, ginger, oak, rosemary (gives woman dominion in home), rowan, St. John's wort, yarrow

Prophetic dreams	Bay, celandine, chamomile, clary, coltsfoot, heliotrope, hops, jasmine, lavender, linden, marigold, mimosa, mugwort, nutmeg, onion, peppermint, sage, St. John's wort, vervain, wormwood
Prosperity	Alfalfa, allspice, almond, ash, banana, basil, bergamot, cashew, cedar, cinquefoil, elder, ginger, ginseng, heliotrope, honesty, honeysuckle, Irish moss, oats, orange, patchouli, pecans, pineapple, pomegranate, poplar, poppy seeds, sage, sassafras, sweet woodruff, tea, tulip, vetivert, wheat
Protection	Agrimony, aloe, angelica, anise seed (evil eye), ash, barley, basil (evil eye), bay leaves, birch, black cohosh root, blackberry, blueberry, broom, bryony, buckwheat, burdock, cactus, caraway seed, carnation, carob, castor, cedar, celandine, chamomile flowers, chrysanthemum, cinnamon, clover flowers, coconut, comfort, corn, cumin, dill, dogwood, eucalyptus,

	fern (from burglars), feverfew (from accident), garlic, hyssop, juniper, lemon grass, marigold, marjoram, mimosa, mint, mustard seed, myrrh, nettle, oak, olive, onion, pansy, parsley, pennyroyal, peony, pepper, periwinkle, pine, primrose, purslane, radish, rag wort, raspberry, rhubarb, rose petals, rosemary, rowan, rue, sage, sandalwood, sloe, snapdragon, St. John's wort, star anise, tamarisk, thistle, turnip, valerian, vervain, violet, willow, wintergreen, witch hazel, wormwood
Psychic powers	Acacia, bay, citron, flax, grass, honeysuckle, lemongrass, mace, marigold, mastic, peppermint, rose, rowan, saffron, thyme (anti-nightmare)
Psychic, prophecy	Althaea leaves, anise seed, calendula flowers, celery seed, cinnamon, flax seed, huckleberry leaves, mugwort, poppy flowers, star anise, tobacco, yarrow
Purification	Broom, cedar, cinnamon, clover flowers (red, white), coconut, eucalyptus, fennel, horseradish, hyssop, lavender, lemon, lemon verbena, lilac, mimosa, myrrh, parsley, peppermint, rosemary, shallot, thyme, tobacco, turmeric,

	valerian, vervain
Removing obstacles	Chicory
Riches	Tea
Romance	Angelica, balm, camphor, carnation, cinnamon, coriander, crocus, eucalyptus, fennel, gardenia, heliotrope, hops, lavender flowers, mimosa, mint, mugwort, myrrh, peppermint, pine, rosemary, rowan, rue, saffron, sage, sandalwood, sassafras, spearmint, thistle, thyme, tobacco, vervain, violet, willow, winter green, wood sorrel, yarrow
Safety during travel	Comfrey, daffodil, feverfew, garlic, heather, Irish moss, juniper, mahogany, mint, mistletoe, mugwort, oak, pennyroyal, quince sccds, rowan, rue, sweet woodruff, wormwood
Sensuality	Juniper berries
Sex/passion	Lemon grass leaves, ginger, lovage root, orris root, rosebuds
Sleep	Elder, hops, lavender, lettuce, linden, passion flower, peppermint, poppy, purslane, rosemary, thyme, valerian, vervain
Spirituality	Cinnamon, frankincense, gardenia, myrrh, sandalwood
Strength	Bay, betony, carnation, comfrey, echinacea, mint, nettle, pennyroyal, saffron, St. John's wort,

	sweet pea, sweet woodruff, tea, thistle
Success	Allspice, basil, balm, cinquefoil, fennel, frankincense, ginger, horse chestnut, pennyroyal, rowan
Wisdom	Cinquefoil, dill, eyebright, flax seed, hazelnuts, iris, mace, mint, mustard seed, rue, sage, savory, spearmint, vanilla
Success	Cinnamon, ginger, marigold, rowan
Treasure finding	Cowslip
Truth	Bluebell
Victory	Woodruff
Virility	Juniper berries
Vision	Coltsfoot, hemp
Ward off evil	Acacia
Ward off sorcery	Dill
Wealth	Camellia, cinquefoil, fern, heliotrope, pomegranate
Wisdom	Iris, sage, sunflower
Wishes	Dandelion, dogwood, ginseng, hazel, peach, pomegranate, sage, sunflower, violet, walnut
Youth	Fern, myrtle, rosemary, vervain

CHAPTER 4

METALS AND GEMSTONES

Metals

Metal amulets are still widely made. With the advent of printing and modern stamping techniques, amulets were mass-produced in metal and paper as pendants, small sheets, or broadsides.

Metal amulets are usually for long-term protection and, in modern times, precious metals are often laminated to protect them from daily wear and tear.

The seven traditional planets each correspond to a specific metal and an amulet reflecting the nature of the planet can be made with that metal. When the amulet is non-metallic, you may choose to attach a chip of the planetary metal to it. Planetary talismans made on metal are generally round. One of the most common ways of using metal for amulets is to engrave planetary images on circles or squares of the metal that corresponds to the intent. Traditionally, metal amulets are prepared on the day of the week that corresponds to the planet that rules the metal.

Saturn – Lead

Lead is easy to work with, but it is toxic and therefore should not come into contact with bare skin. One way of using lead is to use parchment as the base and draw a circle around the symbols with a lead pin. Pewter is often used as an alternative. Saturn amulets are used for protection in general.

Jupiter – Tin

Tin is easy to work with and can be worn as a pendant, engraved with symbols. It can also be etched with acid. It is usually used for money attracting amulets and for luck in general.

Mars – Iron

Iron may be etched with hydrochloric acid, or engraved. Iron is primarily used for healing when you feel under attack, and it is said to increase physical strength. Steel is sometimes used as an alternative.

Sun – Gold

As gold is expensive, bronze or brass are often used as substitutes. Brass is primarily used when the main purpose of the amulet is for protection and to attract money. Pyrite, or fool's gold, is often used for prosperity amulets. Alternatively, gold wire or gold leaf can be used with a parchment amulet. Gold combines well with amber for a success amulet. Gold amulets are used for promoting wisdom, increasing courage and confidence, and success in general.

Venus – Copper

Copper is easy to work with and easy to etch. As an alternative, copper wire can be used with a parchment amulet. Copper is said to work best when worn on the side of the body opposite to your dominant hand. Combining copper with emeralds makes a highly successful love amulet. As copper worn next to the skin can produce a physical effect, it should not be worn for any length of time. Copper amulets are used for attracting love, maintaining health, and drawing luck and prosperity.

Mercury – Mercury

Mercury is liquid, and very toxic. In the past, copper has been used; gold plated using the metal mercury. Brass is often used as a modern alternative. Another cheap alternative is aluminium foil. Mercury amulets are used to improve mental abilities and assure safe travel.

Moon – Silver

Silver is easy to work with, and its price is affordable. It is mainly used for divination, enhancing intuition, dreams and to reflect negativity away.

Silver is also associated with lapis lazuli, jade, pearl, and emerald. When one of these stones is used together with silver, as in a piece of jewellery, it can be used to attract love. Platinum is occasionally used as an alternative. It brings about balance and calm and improves the memory.

Metals are also sometimes associated with the zodiac signs. These are usually related to the planet that rules the sign, and the list of associations can vary slightly in different sources. Here is a common listing:

Aries: Iron
Taurus: Copper
Gemini: Chrome
Cancer: Silver
Leo: Gold
Virgo: Nickel
Libra: Bronze
Scorpio: Steel
Sagittarius: Brass
Capricorn: Pewter
Aquarius: Aluminum
Pisces: Tin

Gemstones

Amulets are frequently made from stones of particular shape or quality. Especially potent are stones from a meteor, which are often magnetic, stones with naturally made holes in them, or geodes, which are spherical stones with a rough exterior and a crystalline interior, sometimes containing water.

Semi-precious stones, such as carnelian or agate, which are often engraved, have been used as amulets for centuries. The gem can be strung and worn or inserted into a piece of jewelry.

Most gems are minerals and therefore the history of gems is tied closely to the history of minerals. Early humanity created tools from quartz and flint. As they progressed into the Bronze Age, metallic minerals were sought after for a variety of uses. Gems were luxury items and appreciated for their beauty.

Gems have always been regarded as mysterious. They were once used in medicine and have always been important as amulets. Paintings in ancient Egyptian tombs depict characters weighing gems, and fashioning lapis and malachite.

Crushed malachite was used as a pigment for painting, as well as eye make-up for ancient Egyptians. In ancient Egypt, the color of the stone was very important to its purpose. Expensive precious stones were often replaced with cheaper stones of a similar color. The most popular stones used were carnelian, green feldspar, lapis lazuli, serpentine, steatite, and turquoise.

In ancient Greece and Rome, gems were believed to hold magical powers and had virtues assigned to them. Not all gems were lucky. The ancient Chinese dreaded onyx, the stone of sadness. It was believed that even entering a mine where it could be found would lead to terrifying dreams, doubts, and disputes.

Much of the traditional gem lore that has survived was passed down through treatises on precious stones called lapidaries. Pliny the Elder, one of Rome's main philosophers, wrote extensively on the powers of gems and their planetary sources, sympathies, and antipathies. His works were very popular throughout the Middle Ages. At the start of the Middle Ages, Isidore of Seville wrote an encyclopaedia called the *Etymologies*. Among other things, he listed the elements, gemstones, and planets to which a color was linked.

The early Christian church opposed magic and condemned engraved talismans, but tolerated the use of medicinal amulets, and developed a symbolism of its own based on the gems of Exodus and the apocalypse. It wasn't until the later part of the seventeenth century that the use of gems was seriously questioned.

One area of confusion is that when looking at traditional sources there is great debate over which stones the writers were really referring to. For example, it's believed that "sapphire" is the English translation of the biblical "sapur," but that "sapur" actually referred to not sapphire but lapis lazuli. The word emerald was often used for many green stones.

Throughout the eleventh century topaz, peridot, and citrine were all referred to as topaz. In the fourteenth century the word "carbuncle" was used to refer to garnets, rubies, and what may have been watermelon tourmaline.

Also, traditional sources often only deal with the most commonly known precious and semiprecious gems and it's hard to find beliefs about more common minerals.

Gems and the Bible

In ancient Judea, the High Priest wore a breastplate set with stones representing the twelve tribes of Israel. Later, this same idea was used to symbolize the twelve Apostles. It was believed that there were twelve sacred gemstones that came from the Mountain of God (where Moses received the Ten Commandments) and were given to Moses.

Many of these same gemstones are listed in *Ezekiel*, Chapter 28 in reference to the King of Tyrus. The book of *Ezekiel* calls them "stones of fire." There are also twelve gemstones listed in *Revelation*, Chapter 21. Although there is confusion surrounding the various names and translations of them, many believe that these gems are the same twelve sacred gemstones.

Emblems of the Twelve Apostles:

Andrew – Blue sapphire

Matthias – Chrysolite

Bartholomew – Red carnelian

Peter – Jasper

James – White chalcedony

Philip – Sardonyx

James-the-less – Topaz

Simeon – Pink hyacinth

John – Emerald

Thaddeus – Chrysoprase

Matthew – Amethyst

Thomas – Beryl (emerald, aquamarine)

Traditional Birthstones

Certain gems have traditionally been associated with different months of the year, and thought lucky or important for people born under their influence. Many cultures associate gems with the signs of zodiac, and others with the months of the year, the selection varying in different countries. The custom of wearing birthstone jewellery started in eighteenth century Poland, and has now spread throughout the world. Early in the twentieth century, the International Gem Society created a new list of birthstones. In the modern list, you find only transparent gems. The ancient list was commonly used by jewlers until 1912. At that time, the American National Retail Jewelers Association (ANRJA) changed the list of birthstones to be more financially beneficial to the jewelry industry. In 1938, the American Gem Society (AGS) adopted the list and added the stone citrine. In 1952, the list was again revised, and in 2003, tanzanite was accepted as an alternative December birthstone.

International Gem Society birthstones.

MONTH	MODERN	ANCIENT
January	Garnet	Garnet
February	Amethyst	Amethyst
March	Aquamarine	Bloodstone
April	Diamond	Diamond
May	Emerald	Emerald

June	Alexandrite	Pearl
July	Ruby	Ruby
August	Peridot	Sardonyx
September	Sapphire	Sapphire
October	Rose Zircon	Tourmaline or Opal
November	Golden Topaz	Topaz
December	Blue Zircon	Turquoise or Lapis

Birthstones are based on two main systems – the astrological, where each stone is related to a planet according to its color and properties, and Biblical associations. The table below gives birthstones according to different systems. The stones are allocated to months, and the relevant zodiac sign is the one that begins around the 21st of that month.

Birthstones from different cultures

Month Birthstones	Arabic Birthstones	Hebrew Birthstones	Hindu Birthstones	Italian Birthstones	Polish Birthstones	Roman Birthstones	Russian Birthstones
January Aquarius	Garnet	Garnet	Serpent stone *	Jacinth Garnet	Garnet	Garnet	Garnet Hyacinth
February Pisces	Amethyst	Amethyst	Chandrakanta *	Amethyst	Amethyst	Amethyst	Amethyst
March Aries	Bloodstone	Jasper (Sometimes bloodstone)	The gold Siva-linga *	Jasper	Bloodstone	Bloodstone	Jasper
April Taurus	Sapphire	Sapphire	Diamond	Sapphire	Diamond	Sapphire	Sapphire

May Gemini	Emerald	Agate Carnelian Chalcedony	Emerald	Agate	Emerald	Agate	Emerald
June Cancer	Agate Chalcedony Pearl	Emerald	Pearl	Emerald	Agate Chalcedony	Emerald	Agate Chalcedony
July Leo	Carnelian	Onyx	Sapphire	Onyx	Ruby	Onyx	Ruby Sardonyx
August Virgo	Sardonyx	Carnelian	Ruby	Carnelian	Sardonyx	Carnelian	Alexandrite
September Libra	Chrysolite	Chrysolite	Zircon	Chrysolite	Sardonyx	Sardonyx	Chrysolite
October Scorpio	Aquamarine	Aquamarine	Coral	Beryl	Aquamarine	Aquamarine	Beryl
November Sagittarius	Topaz	Topaz	Cat's-eye	Topaz	Topaz	Topaz	Topaz
December Capricorn	Ruby	Ruby	Topaz	Ruby	Turquoise	Ruby	Turquoise Chrysoprase

* Unknown

Stones for Particular Types of Amulets

Whatever type of amulet you wish to create, you will have a choice of several suitable stones. Traditionally, it's recommended that you buy the best stone that you can afford. It can be better to buy a good quality cheaper stone, than a poor quality version of an expensive stone. It isn't necessary to use a large stone – a small chip can be enough when added to other materials in your amulet. You can wear your chosen stone set in jewelry or carry it along with other materials relevant to the purpose of your amulet.

Associations of Stones

Calmness and balance	Amethyst, ametrine, aquamarine, citrine, coral, diamond, jade, malachite, pink tourmaline, tanzanite, zircon
Happiness	Agate, amethyst, calcite, diamond, jade
Intuition	Lapis lazuli, moonstone, tanzanite
Love	Jade, malachite, red jasper, rose quartz
Love and friendship	Alexandrite, amber, amethyst, emerald, moonstone, pink tourmaline, sapphire, topaz
Luck	Alexandrite, amber, aventurine, opal, pearl, turquoise.
Mental clarity	Amber, lapis lazuli, moonstone, silver, smoky quartz, topaz
Productivity	Agate, garnet, opal
Protection	Garnet, obsidian, onyx, quartz crystal in a white bag
Prosperity	Gold tiger's eye in a green bag, jade, peridot
Self esteem	Aventurine, carnelian, diamond, emerald, garnet
Serenity	Amethyst, blue lace agate, jade, quartz crystal
Strength and confidence	Agate, amber, aquamarine, carnelian, diamond, garnet, iolite, malachite, onyx, opal, ruby, sapphire, topaz (blue)
Wealth	Alexandrite, calcite, emerald, jade, opal, pearl, peridot, ruby, sapphire, topaz, tourmaline
Wisdom	Coral, jade, pearl

The Qualities of Gemstones Commonly Used in Amulets

Gemstone	Description	Month	Planet	Attributes	Legend
Adamant	A lustrous diamond. The word adamant means "invincible" or "impenetrable", and was applied to extremely hard minerals.	January	Sun /Mars	Steadfastness.	
Agate	Brown Frequently formed in the vugs of volcanic rocks. A form of chalcedony.	January	Moon Mercury	Brown agate has been used to drive away fevers, epilepsy, and madness as well as to stop the flow of rheum in the eye and reduce menstruation. Blue laced agate promotes feminine qualities, gentleness. Black Agate protects against envy; makes athletes invincible. Green agate combats eye diseases. Gray agate prevents colic. Red agate protects against stings of spiders and scorpions, and against storms and lightning. Agate is mood lifting and used as an amulet to guard against the evil eye.	The name agate comes from the Sicilian river formerly called Achates. Early civilizations, including the ancient Egyptians, used agate for seals and protective talismans. Hebrew name of Shebo.
Alexandrite	Red to green	June (health)		Aids in centering, enhances self-esteem and feelings of joy. Often substituted for pearl.	

| Amazonite | Aqua-green | | | Enhances and stimulates thoughts, balances the emotions. Self expression. | |

| Amber | Technically not a stone at all but fossilized resin, only the pearl predates its use as a gem. | | Mercury | Aids in enhancing and balancing moods, obtaining mental clarity, and confidence. It can also be used to purify or detoxify. Rids depression, lifts the spirit. Reduces fever. Amber preserves the wearer from rheumatism, toothache, headache, rickets, and jaundice. | Amber was mixed with honey for earache or failure of sight. Amber dust relieved pains in the stomach and helped the kidneys, liver, and intestines. The smell of burnt amber aided women in labor. Amber beads have been found in prehistoric sites, and amber is believed to have been traded before 2000 BCE. In Greek legend, amber was a concretion of tears shed at the death of Meleager by his sisters. In Scandinavian mythology, it was the tears shed by Freya when Odin wandered out into the world. To the Chinese it was the soul of the tiger transformed into the mineral after death. A goblet made of amber was believed to detect poison. |

| Amethyst | Purple variety of quartz | February (sincerity)

 Scorpio

 November | Jupiter and Mars Water | Used against insomnia. Absorbs, purifies and transmutes negativity. Stimulates spiritual growth, initiates understanding and calms the mind. Cleanses, to cure gout. A calming influence, used for clarity, and protection from sorcerers and thieves. It is said to help you recognize the truth in yourself and others. | Amethyst has been held in the same value as diamond. It can be found among crown jewels and in the rings of religious leaders. Amethyst means not drunken and would protect the wearer from drunkenness. The ancient Egyptians considered the amethyst a stone of the intellect and wisdom. In the Renaissance, it was engraved with the image of bear for protection. Amethyst is one |

Name	Color/Description	Month/Zodiac	Planet	Properties	History/Legend
					of the stones in the Breastplate of Judgment of Aaron, described in the Bible.
Apatite	Neon turquoise			Balances, integrates, aids in meditation and creativity.	
Aquamarine	Aqua	March (courage)		Inspiration. Promotes inner peace, stabilizes, balances, purifies, clears thinking, purifies confidence. Draws affectionate feelings from others. Used by sailors for safe passage.	
Aventurine	Deep sparkling green		Venus	Promotes creative insight, independence and originality, stabilizes and balances healing, especially emotional pain, promotes balance, love, prosperity, and truth. Increases libido, confidence, and gratitude. Used for good results in gambling.	The Chinese highly prized this stone, and held it in higher esteem than jade.
Beryl	An important mineral species that includes aquamarine and emerald. Transparent varieties in white, green, blue, yellow, or pink are valued as gems.	Libra October January	Venus	Green beryl is used to overcome eye diseases. Yellowish beryl was prescribed for jaundice and a bad liver and to clear and soothe the emotions. Beryl gives marital harmony, protects against gossip, harmony, courage, and strength, dispels fear, brings good luck and good fortune, and increases the intellect and creativity. It also pro-	Beryl was the gem connected to the biblical tribe of Gad, the tribe of good fortune. It was associated with fortune telling and in ancient times women gazed into a beryl sphere to foretell the future. Beryl is one of the stones in the Breastplate of Judgment of Aaron, described in the Bible. Legends say that aquamarine is the treasure of mermaids, with the power to keep sailors safe at sea. A dream of

				tects travellers from danger	aquamarine means that you will meet new friends.
Bloodstone			Mars Aries or Scorpio,	Fame and long life. Soothes the mind, relieves depression, aids in grounding energy, calming, and increasing wealth and prosperity. Encourages victory in competition, attracts wealth, increases crop yield.	Ancient Babylonians carved symbols in bloodstone, or heliotrope, which allowed the future to be foretold. Later it became a Christian symbol, the red spots representing the blood of Christ diffusing in the green stone.
Carbuncle	Dark red garnet		Sun	Gives self-confidence, constancy and energy. Protects young children	
Carnelian	A deep rusty red, translucent stone. A variety of chalcedony.	Taurus May	Mars, sometimes Saturn Fire	Bestows courage and eloquence upon the wearer, especially recommended for those speaking in public. Helps to relax and bring strength, protection, and determination. Promotes peace and harmony, and dispels depression and grief. Assists with inner strength and courage, grounds energies to the present, stimulates aids in gaining confidence, strength, precision, and ability to analyze, and helps to restore appetite. Said to affect fertility. Protects against ruin and betrayal.	Worn on the hand in ancient Egypt to still anger, jealousy, envy, and hatred.

Cat's-eye	Chrysoberyl (cymophane)			A stabilizing influence, opening one to a sense of self worth and allowing forgiveness.	Traditionally, it was washed in milk and the liquid drunk by a husband. Should his wife commit adultery after his departure, no child would be born of the illicit union. In Arabic tradition, it was believed that it could make the wearer invisible in battle.
	A translucent, yellowish, cloudy stone.				
Chalcedony	Chrysoprase	July Cancer		Prevention and cure of melancholy. Protects against drowning.	The Greeks and Romans used it in their seals and signets. It was said to have the power to confer invisibility on the one who wore it. In older texts, the word chrysoprase was used when chrysoberyl was meant. It was believed that a thief about to be hanged or beheaded could escape if he held a bit of chrysoprase in his mouth. Chalcedony was sacred to Diana, and connected to victory in arguments and battles
	Apple green and slightly fluorescent. A quartz that has a cloudy, non-crystalline appearance, such as agate. Its common colors are blue-gray, white (cream), and redbrown.				
Charoite	Purple			Brings fears into consciousness to dissolve fear patterns, enhances courage and strength leading to greater awareness of purpose on earth. Protects against depression.	
Chrysolite	Yellow/green		Sun Venus	Leads to greater inner peace, amplifies thoughts	
	In Victorian times, it included chrysoberyls and can also refer to peridot.				

Citrine	Golden yellow A yellow quartz, tra- ditionally known as a merchant's stone.	November	Mercury	Gives glowing emo- tional warmth, helps the rational mind, and energizes. Attracts abundance, aids in problem solv- ing, mental and emotional clarity, confidence, and dis- cipline. Reduces fear and depression, and aids in diges- tion. Represents fidelity. Kept with loose change helps ensure prosperity. Aids memory and motivates writers. Keeps sickness away and protects when traveling.	
Coral	Red, black, white, pink.		Venus	Protects against evil eye. Used to over- come sterility, for sea travel, marital harmony, and pro- tection. Increases compassion and sensitivity. Black coral dispels nega- tivity. White coral relieves stress, calms.	Often given to new-born babies for protection. Christian painters of the fourteenth century often represented the child Jesus as holding corals in his hand. Coral is one of the seven treasures in Buddhist scriptures and Tibetan Lamas use coral rosaries.
Danburite	Clear			Activates intellect, helps to balance individual identity.	
Diamond	Clear	April (innocence)	Sun	Symbol of power, strength, innocence and incorruptibility, longevity, constancy, and good fortune. Fosters unity and love, trust and fideli- ty. Aids in creativity, prosperity, and love. Can be used in place of all other gems. Drives away madness and pro- tects against ghosts and sorcery.	There was an old Persian belief that the diamond was a source of sin and sorrow.

Emerald	The bright green variety of beryl.	May Taurus September Virgo	Venus Mercury	Ensures loyalty and improves memory. Enhances mental wisdom and healing, growth, peace, love, harmony, patience, fidelity, and honesty. Reduces depression and aids in sleep. Helps success in love, and discovery of false friends. Used as a protection at sea. Helps the wearer deal with emotional distur- bances and trauma, increases intellect and creativity, strengthens memory.	This was often a sacred symbol of fertility and growth and it is said that some emeralds can be used to call on the dark angels and spirits. There is an Indian tale about emeralds originating from fireflies in moonlight. Emerald is one of the stones in the Breastplate of Judgment of Aaron, described in the Bible.
Fluorite	Violet, blue, green, yellow			Aids in focusing, cleansing, and purifying. Conducts and aligns energies, and opens the way for other stones. Prepares and balances.	
Garnet	A transparent stone which is usually a darkish plum red.	January (constancy)	Mars Sun	Encourages good health and sexual desire, enhances the wearer's imagination. Symbolizes fire, faith, courage, truth, grace, compassion, con- stancy, and fidelity. Dissipates sadness, controls inconti- nence, and averts evil thoughts and dreams. Gives ability to make deep and lasting friendships, activates deep eter- nal love, grounds and protects. Exchanged as gifts between friends to demonstrate their affection for each other and to ensure that they meet again.	Used as bullets by some tribes in the past. Believed to contain a flare of lightning inside it, garnet was also thought to keep one safe from lightning strikes. It has been worn throughout the ages for protection while traveling.

Garnet-Color Change	Pink to golden raisin		Fosters commitment, balances and integrates emotions.	
Hematite	Opaque with a metallic luster, often black or silvery though having a blood-red streak and showing blood-red when cut in thin slices.	Mars	Healing, grounding, strengthens. Gives success in law suits.	It was believed that when warriors rubbed their bodies with hematite, they became invulnerable. The ancient Egyptians used this stone to treat hysteria and as ornamental objects placed inside their tombs.
Jet	Black		Heals epilepsy, toothache, headache, and glandular swellings.	
Iolite	Violet-blue/gray		Transforms intellectual knowledge into intuition and true wisdom. Enhances will power and unselfish energy, gives insight and sense of direction.	When the legendary Viking mariners sailed the ocean, they used thin pieces of iolite as the world's first polarizing filter.
Hyacinth	Semi-precious stone also known as jacinth. It is a lustrous orange-yellow, orange-red, or yellow-brown type of zircon. Sometimes, topaz and garnets of this color are also referred to as hyacinth and a hyacinth opal is one that is yellow or orange.	Sagittarius Sun	Friendship and healing. Provides the wearer with wisdom, honor, and riches. It balances the emotions and enhances self-esteem and unity. Worn as an amulet by travelers to protect against accident and injury on the journey. Also used to stop the wearer from being stuck by lightning.	Jacinth is one of the stones in the Breastplate of Judgment of Aaron, described in the Bible. If the stone loses luster it is said to warn of danger. Hindu poets tell of the Kalpa Tree, the ultimate gift to the gods, which was a glowing tree covered with gemstone fruit and leaves of hyacinth. In the middle ages, it was said to aid sleep, bring prosperity, and promote honor and wisdom in its owner.

Stone	Color / Planet	Month	Planet	Properties	Lore
Jade	Moss green Neptune			It draws luck, health, long life, love, and prosperity. Promotes inner assurance, soothes nervous energy, harmonizes with all wealth, health, longevity, wisdom, justice, courage, balance, fidelity, love, and peace. A relaxing, harmonizing, cooling stone said to stimulate profound thought and healing meditation. Jade is an ancient love-attracting stone. Good for business.	Jade is sometimes placed in the bathtub as a calming influence. Wearing the stone is believed to help kidney, heart, and stomach problems.
Jasper	Green, brown, red. A variety of chalcedony.	August Leo	Mars Venus	Brown jasper directs energies towards the body. Red jasper attracts a love affair or maintains passion. All colors of jasper aid in grounding energy and healing. It also helps bring hidden thoughts, fears, and hopes to surface. The stones are reported to get more personal and stronger the longer they are worn, helping us attract what we need rather than what we may want.	Jasper is one of the stones in the Breastplate of Judgment of Aaron, described in the Bible. It has been said that it originated when Christ's blood fell to the ground and was scattered on the rocks under the Cross. Many early Christians wore it to remind them of Christ's sacrifice. Stones made of jasper have been treasured throughout history for their value as an amulet by all ancient peoples including the Native Americans and one of the tribes of Israel. In ancient times, it was used in seals and to ward off drought.
Kunzite	Lilac pink			Aids in external expression of internalized self-love, and promotes tolerance, acceptance and peace. Balances mind and heart.	

Labradorite	Gray with flashes of blue and green.			nspires expanding consciousness and greater self-aware-ness.	
Lapis Lazuli	Royal blue	December (prosperity) January	Venus Saturn Neptune	Enhances psychic abilities, helpful to spiritual teachers. Increases mental clarity, virility, and calm. Expels melancholy, harmonizes and stabilizes, relieves anxiety and shyness.	Vivid blue, used since 1300 BCE. Used by Egyptians for cosmetics and painting. Was believed to be a sacred stone, buried with the dead to protect and guide them in the after-life.
Larimar	Blue/green/white			Calms emotions, promotes harmony between heart and mind, and enhances verbal expression.	
Lavender Strawberry Quartz	Lavender with sparkles			Transmutes energy into spiritual growth and enhances self-esteem. Calming, leads to lessening of anxiety.	
Marchasite			Mercury Venus Moon	Aids in grounding energy, mental clari-ty, concentration, memory, sleep, con-fidence, and willpow-er. Helps relieve anxiety and stress.	
Malachite	Vivid green			Good for sea travel exploring. Gives inspiration and heightens intuition. Amplifies moods, provides protection, and creates calm and peace. Clears subconscious blocks and aids one's sleep.	Crushed malachite was used as a pigment for painting, as well as eye make-up for ancient Egyptians. In the Middle Ages, malachite was worn to protect from black magic and sorcery.

Moldavite	Green			Aids in spiritual evolution, grounds light for healing the planet, and enhances dreams and intuition. Cleanses blockages, and energizes.	
Moonstone	Pearly white	June (health)	Moon Water	Protective for women and babies. It helps develop psychic awareness, soothes and balances emotions. Encourages inner awareness, reflects reality, and relieves stress. Helps emotional balance, and enhances gracefulness. Aids in relieving menstrual pains and helps balance female hormones.	Some legends say it was formed out of the rays of the moon. Others claim you can see the future in a moonstone during a waning moon. Still others say it's a propitious stone for lovers with the power to make the wearer faithful. Moonstone is said to guard against the evil eye.
Morganite	Soft pink			Encourages love and helps maintain wisdom and patience.	
Opal	Iridescent with play of color	October (hope) February	Moon Cancer	Fidelity. Develops joy, intuition and creativity. Diversifies or scatters, amplifies traits, yet balances. Aids in finding love and passion. Heightens spontaneity, visualisation, healing, and dreams. Clarifies and absorbs emotions.	The opal has long since emerged from the slight cloud of disfavor due to a belief that it was in some way associated with ill-luck. This idea found an opponent in Queen Victoria, whose influence did much to make opals fashionable. They have become favorite bridal gifts. The ancient Romans called it *cupid paederos*, "child beautiful as love," regarding it as a symbol of hope and purity. In Arab lore, opals are the remnants of lightning strikes to the ground, and the flashes in the stone are captured lightning. It wasn't until the nineteenth century that the opal became known

						as a gem of ill omen and was connected with misfortunes of European royalty.
Onyx	Black	January	Saturn Earth		Stabilization, comfort, and faith. Protects, balances, grounds energy, and absorbs intense feelings.	Onyx, the stone of sadness, was dreaded by the ancient Chinese. It was believed that entering a mine where it could be found would lead to terrifying dreams, doubts, and disputes. Onyx is said to absorb the thought and energy patterns around it, keeping a silent record of events, feelings, and memories.
Pearl	Cream with overtones and iridescence	June (health)			Chastity and purity. Helps intuition and divination, and is an aid to friendship, safety, hope and prosperity. Creates beauty and harmony from discord, activates purity and sacrificial love. Aids in emotional balancing, and stimulates creativity.	
Peridot	Yellowish green	August (wedded bliss)	Mercury		Alleviates spiritual fear, balances the physical body, clears mental fatigue. Encourages prosperity, growth, and wealth. Relieves negative emotions such as anger, jealousy, fear, anxiety, and depression. Dispels female betrayal; encourages friendships.	Peridot, or olivine, was first mined by Egyptians in the Red Sea area. A favorite of the Pharaohs, peridot had the power to dispel dark forces. Peridot has been mined as a gemstone for an estimated four thousand years or better, and is mentioned in the Bible under the Hebrew name of *pitdah*. Peridot gems, along with other gems, were probably used in the fabled Breastplates of the Jewish High Priest.

Phenakite	Milky clear			Centers, aids in expanding conscious awareness, and enhances relationships.	
Quartz Crystal Moon	Clear	April (innocence)	Mercury Air.	Helps to focus and sharpen the mind as well as to help you communicate more clearly. Can aid in creative thinking and writing. Promotes clarity of mental vision, amplifies and balances energies.	Extensively used among the Romans for the manufacture of drinking-cups and similar vessels, and for personal ornaments. Balls of rock-crystal were carried by Roman ladies to keep their hands cool during the summer heat.
Raspberry Rhodolite Garnet	Raspberry pink			Balances emotions, fosters greater awareness and cooperation.	
Rhodochrosite	Pink with white bands			Integrates spiritual and physical energies, releases emotional stress.	
Rose Quartz	Light pink			Opens the heart to soft, loving emotions, calms.	
Ruby	Red	July (contentment)	Sun	To bring about a very deep and pure love affair. Promotes free flowing, divine love and courage, and energizes. Used for **love**, confidence, courage, vitality, and passion. Warms and soothes the soul, helps success, intensifies all emotions. Protects your house and land from storms and lightning. Dispels sadness and love troubles.	According to Burmese legend, rubies were hatched from eggs laid deep in Earth. A woman wishing to prove her virtue should wear the ruby on her left hand, as there it would control amorous desire.

Rutilated Quartz	Clear with golden needles			Contains magnetic force fields for currents of energy. Counters against radiation, enhances agelessness, encourages optimism.	
Sapphire	Blue Sapphire is a variety of the mineral corundum. Can be any color except red.	September (clear thinking)	Venus	Purity, used for engaged couples, to encourage a peaceful and happy life. Provides protection, luck, peace of mind, and thwarts disease. Promotes insight and instant knowing, enhances creative mind. Symbolizes truth, sincerity, love, friendship, and faithfulness.	Early Christian theologians believed gazing at blue sapphire would elevate one's thoughts from earthly to heavenly matters. In the sixth century, it became a ruling that every cardinal should wear a sapphire ring on his right hand. Sapphire is one of the stones in the Breastplate of Judgment of Aaron, described in the Bible. Ancient Persians believed sapphires gave heaven its blue color, and some believed that the heavens formed a huge sapphire to act as a support for the earth, and its reflection colored the sky. Tradition holds that Moses was given the ten commandments on tablets of sapphire. Because sapphires represent divine favor, they were the gemstone of choice for kings and high priests.
Sapphire-Color Change	Lavender to teal			Leads to joy and peace of mind, balances energy, integrates the mind.	
Sard	Light or dark brown chalcedony			Promotes peace, happiness, forgiveness, compassion, and fidelity. Attracts love, while clearing anger, resentment, fear and guilt.	

Sardonyx	A semi-precious stone that is formed by two layers, a type of quartz. Reddish brown or white.	April Aries	Helps promote healthy relation-ships, and helps to balance heaven and earth.	Sardonyx is one of the stones in the Breastplate of Judgement of Aaron, described in the Bible. It is frequently carved to make intricate cameos and seals. Sardonyx was highly valued in Rome for seals, because it was said to never stick to the wax.
Smoky Quartz	Grayish brown		A stone with power-ful white light ener-gy, softens negative thought forms, enhances aware-ness of sounds.	
Spessartite Garnet	Reddish orange		Helps with growth, balance and analyti-cal processes.	
Spinel	Pink, violet		Renews energy, enhances appear-ance, energizes beauty.	
Strawberry Quartz	Pink with golden sparkles		Enhances self-esteem, aids in reducing anxiety, contains energy fields activating uni-versal love.	
Sugilite	Royal purple		Aids in opening the third eye, integrates spiritual energies, links the mind to the body, and grounds the purple ray.	
Tanzanite	Royal indigo		Helps the will to fos-ter achievement, assists in exploring aspects of the self.	
Tiger's-eye	An opaque brown stone, with streaks of darker brown,		Strength and inde-pendence. Aids busi-ness start-ups,	

67

	black and golden-yellow.			willpower, confidence, assurance, and clear thinking. Relieves anxiety. Offers protection, courage, energy, and luck.	It is said that Roman soldiers wore tiger's-eye for protection in battle.
Topaz	Yellow	November (fidelity) June Gemini	Moon Jupiter Sun Mercury	Love and affection. Topaz has special powers transmitted to the wearer; long life, beauty and intelligence will wax and wane with the phases of the Moon. Source of strength, hope and expansiveness. Balances emotions and energies, rejuvenates, warms and dispels fears. Aids mental clarity, focus, and confidence. Helps mood swings and relieves worries, depression, fear, insomnia, exhaustion, and depression. Gives focus, tranquility, and creative expression. Drives away sadness, strengthens the intellect, and grants courage. Protection against hatred and revenge.	Early lapidaries cite topaz as a stone capable of cooling boiling water, curing eye disease and gall, dispelling night terrors, lessening anger and lechery, and being able to cure cowardice. It was also said to be a protection against untimely death. Topaz is also considered precious by African bushmen and is used in ceremonies for healing and contacting spirits. St. Hildegarde claimed that she read prayers in a darkened chapel by the light emanating from a topaz. Formerly, mariners turned to it when they had no daylight, or moon to direct their course. Topaz is one of the stones in the Breastplate of Judgment of Aaron, described in the Bible. Ancient Egyptians said topaz was colored with the glow from Ra, the sun god, and they used it as a good luck charm to protect against harm. The Romans associated topaz with Jupiter, their god of the sun. The Greeks believed it made its wearer invisible in time of trouble, and they thought it increased strength. Topaz was believed by many to hold other magical powers.

Legend has it that Topaz dispels all enchantment and helps to improve eyesight as well! Topaz was also said to change color in the presence of poisoned food or drink.

Tourmalinated Quartz	Clear with black needles.			Creates a balance of light and darkness, breaks negative habit patterns, transforms negative energies.	
Tourmaline	Pink, green, blue	October		Balances polarities of energy, leads to greater awareness, creates equilibrium, and harmonizes.	If rubbed or heated, it will develop a static charge that attracts lightweight particles to its surface. Tourmaline was recognized as a gem in Europe in 1703 when Dutch traders brought it back from the East. It has been used by both African and Australian shamans, and was used to provide direction toward that which was "good"; it was also recognized as a "teller" stone, providing insight during times of struggle and "telling" who and/or what is causing trouble.
Tsavorite Garnet	Intense green			Stimulates knowledge in higher planes, assists with sensitivity.	
Turquoise	Turquoise	December (prosperity)	Venus Sun	Brings good fortune and physical well-being. Multi-purpose. Balances polarities of energy, creates equilibrium, and harmonizes. Provides physical protection, enhances creative force, and is a general healer, relieving	Turquoise is freely employed in the decoration of religious objects. The Tibetans believe that turquoise will turn pale if the person wearing it has a downward turn in fortune or health; a loss of color is considered portentous of coming evil.

			many negative emotions. Increases psychic connections, divination skills, communication, creativity, and serenity. Uplifting, sooths and calms. Protects against hatred and revenge. Protects against danger when traveling.
Zircon	Sparkling blue	December (prosperity)	Balances virtue, helps with hardiness, intuition and purity.

CHAPTER 5

SHAPES AND IMAGES

Simple amulets can be transcribed with a shape or image representing the purpose that the amulet is being put to. An alternative is to actually make the amulet in a specific shape. Some of the most common amulets are those against the evil eye, and eye-shaped amulets are often seen in Greece and Turkey. It was common in the Middle Ages for treatises to give images of the designs to be placed on amulets.

The ancient Assyrians, Egyptians, Babylonians, Arabs, and Hebrews placed great importance in amulets and used a variety of images and symbols. For example, a frog protected fertility, ankhs everlasting life, and scarab resurrection. Hebrews wore crescent moons to ward off evil.

Two universal symbols are eyes and phallic symbols. Eyes are used to protect against evil spirits and phallic symbols against evil. The phallic symbol, represented by horns and hands, is also used as protection against the evil eye. In modern witchcraft, the most powerful amulet is the silver pentacle, the symbol of the craft.

Commonly Used Symbols and Their Meanings

Acorn – Power, fertility, survival. Benefits baby or young child. Attracts the opposite sex.

Anchor – Hope.

Ankh – Good health, fertility, and strengthens the psychic powers.

Arrow – Mortality and protection against enemies, bad luck, and jealousy. Used to protect the home against burglars. Protection against illness.

Bear – Helps during childbirth and increases physical strength.

Bee – Productivity.

Bull – Fertility in women and virility in men. Protects the wearer against maledictions, procures the favor of magistrates.

Buttercup – Cheerfulness.

Butterfly – Resurrection and eternal life.

Cat – Improves night vision, protects against evil entities, or makes secret wishes come true.

Circle – Eternity.

Cock – Vigilance and protection against the evil eye.

Clover or Shamrock – Luck.

Corn – Productivity and fruitfulness.

Cow – Fruitfulness and productivity

Crab – Fertility and attracts love.

Crescent Moon – Fertility and to attract a lover.

Dolphin – Protects against accidents when traveling by boat.

Dove – Peace.

Dragon – Controls water.

Eagle – Swiftness.

Egg – Love and fertility.

Eye – Protection against the evil eye.

Feather – Supernatural powers, communication, healing, and hospitality. Good for business.

Fern – Sincerity.

Fish – Fertility, prosperity, and protection. Wealth and increase.

Frog – Friendship, reconciliation.

Goat – Fertility.

Hands – Farewell, or if clasped, fidelity

Hare – A creature with supernatural powers widely associated with lunar deities, and particularly popular in China. The markings on the Moon are said to resemble a hare. Chinese legends told of a white hare that lived on the Moon, pounding an elixir of immortality with a pestle and mortar. The hare is a symbol of longevity, fertility, and victory over lust. Today a rabbit's foot is often used for the same purpose.

Heart – Love.

Holly – Foresight

Horn – Protects against evil. When worn by a man, the horn increases sex appeal and virility.

Horse – Courage.

Horseshoe – A symbol of protection since the Middle Ages, placed on or over the door of many kinds of buildings, or worn as an amulet. In modern times, it has been stated that the horseshoe should be placed open end up so that the good luck doesn't run out. However, traditionally it is used with the open end down as it represents the symbol used for the north node of the Moon, ♌, which represents success.

Key – Learning. Two keys give remembrance of things past and foresight of things to come.

Knot – Binds what is good and hinders that which isn't

Lion – Courage, boldness, and nobility. To cure shyness, overcome enemies, protect against danger while traveling, and strengthen emotions.

Owl – Knowledge and wisdom.

Peacock – Immortality. Peacock feathers are considered unlucky around children and unmarried girls.

Phallus – Virility and protection against the evil eye.

Pig – In ancient Egypt, sow and piglets formed a popular amulet, worn to make women fertile. Protection against the evil eye.

Pomegranate – Fertility.

Pyramid – Improves work habits, increases psychic powers, or attracts good luck. Ram – Fertility.

Rod – Power.

Rose – Silence.

Salmon – Regeneration and life.

Scorpion – Repels evil and negative forces, and guards against enemies.

Seal of Solomon – Also known as the Star of David, the Seal of Solomon is a powerful symbol with many mystical and magical qualities. As an amulet, it offers protection against enemies and brings good luck.

Serpent – Wisdom.

Shark – Strength.

Skull – Protection against the evil eye.

Snake – Increases wisdom and sexual powers.

Snail – Love.

Spider – Shrewdness in business and quickness of sight

Sun – Success and fame.

Swallow – Good luck.

Sword – Justice and strength.

Toadstool – Phallic symbol.

Tortoise – Longevity.

Wishbone – Good luck and to make wishes and dreams come true.

The Evil Eye

Many believe that some people can bestow a curse on victims by the malevolent gaze of their magical eye. The effects on victims vary. They can be afflicted with bad luck or suffer disease.

Some cultures hold that the evil eye is an involuntary jinx is cast unintentionally by people unlucky to be cursed with the power to bestow. Others hold that it is called forth by the sin of envy. The curse is usually unintentional and caused by praising and looking enviously at the victim. Belief in the evil eye is not necessarily associated with witchcraft or sorcery, though evil eye was something Church inquisitors were instructed to look for.

Belief in the evil eye is strongest in the Middle East, Asia and Europe, especially the Mediterranean region. In some areas where light-colored eyes are rare, people with blue eyes are feared. Others believe that green-eyed individuals can also cause the evil eye, or those with connected eyebrows. A common rural belief is that babies whose breastfeeding is interrupted and then resumed will have the ability to cast the evil eye. The evil eye features in Islamic folk religion. It is also significant in Jewish folklore. In Latin, the evil eye was *fascinum*, the origin of the word "to fascinate."

The belief in the evil eye is thought to have originated in Sumeria. It is mentioned in the Old Testament, and acknowledged by modern Arabs, Jews, and Christians. The belief extends eastward to India, westward to Spain and Portugal, northward to Scandinavia and Britain, and southward into North Africa. Belief in the evil eye isn't completely universal. China has no evil-eye belief – nor does Korea, Burma, Taiwan, Indonesia, Thailand, Sumatra, Vietnam, Cambodia, Laos, Japan, Australia, New Zealand, North America, South America, or any of Africa south of the Sahara.

Its origins may have its roots in fear of strangers. Various rituals have developed to counteract the effects of the evil eye, such as defusing the praise, putting spit or dirt on a child who is praised, averting the gaze of strangers, or reciting some verses from the Bible or the Quran.

Some folklorists believe that the evil eye belief is rooted in primate biology (dominance and submission are shown by gazing and averting the gaze) and relates to our dislike of staring.

Some cultures refrain from complimenting the parents of a newborn child for fear of risking the evil eye. For this reason, some traditional families keep mother and child in seclusion for the first forty days after the birth. Those who are aware of the dangers of praise often spit after paying a compliment. In the West, young boys were often dressed as girls to fool the evil eye, boy children being more valuable.

Attempts to ward off the curse of the evil eye has resulted in a number of talismans and amulets. Balls or disks painted with a blue circle and a concentric black circle inside to represent an evil eye, are common in the Middle East. The large eyes often seen painted at the prows of Mediterranean boats are there to ward off the evil eye. In ancient Rome, people believed that phallic charms and ornaments offered proof against the evil eye. Sexual gestures were also made to prevent the evil eye, for example, a fist with the index and little finger extended or a fist with the thumb pressed between the index and middle fingers. Small blue or black glass beads, decorated with a black spot inside a white circle to resemble the iris of an eye, are popular for pinning to clothing.

There are innumerable amulets worn against the effects of the evil eye, and the design varies from one area to another. The simplest are threads or cords, often red. Sometimes the eye is combined with another element, such as a hand or horseshoe.

In Greece and Turkey, the most common form is the blue glass eye charm, which mirrors back the blue of the evil eye. Among the ancient Egyptians the eye of the god Horus was worn, usually made of a blue stone. In the Middle East, turquoise blue beads are used to protect live-stock from the evil eye. In India, cord charms strung with a blue bead are placed on newborn babies; when the cord decays and breaks and the blue bead is lost, the child is considered old enough to have escaped the dangers of the evil eye. Red is employed against the eye in some regions, instead of blue.

Among the Kalbeliya Gypsies of India, the mirroring back of the evil eye takes the form of ornate multi-colored mirror charms, which are crocheted, braided, and wrapped with beads, buttons, and tassels. The Italians use an amulet that looks like a long, twisted animal horn. In Europe, the horseshoe offers protection against the evil eye, and is nailed to houses and barns as protection. Any protective amulet can be used to combat the effects of the evil eye.

CHAPTER 6

THE USE OF COLOR

Throughout history, civilizations have associated colors with symbolic meanings and the impact of color on mood is widely recognized. Color has played an enormous role in past civilizations through ritual, home decoration, body ornaments, and body paint. It has also played a vital part in the diagnosis and treatment of illness.

In the past, colors were associated with disease because disease produced color. Plants, flowers, minerals, and elixirs were thought to be more effective when their hues resembled the pallor of the flesh or sores on it. Therefore, red, yellow, and black had great medicinal value, as they were identified with fever, plague, and death.

Color has always fascinated humanity and it has always been regarded as one of life's greatest mysteries. However, in many languages few colors bear names. The highest number of basic color terms has been found to exist in English, where there are eleven: black, white, red, orange, yellow, green, blue, purple, pink, gray and brown. Other colors have names based on items that are examples of them, such as avocado, grape, peach, tan, gold.

Ancient Egyptians believed that red, yellow, and blue corresponded to the body, soul, and spirit. The Indian Ayurveda and Chinese systems of medicine both refer to the science of color as a power that can vitalize, enlighten, animate, heal, supply, inspire, and fulfil. They maintain that each individual is influenced by the seven major rays or the colors of the rainbow – red, orange, yellow, green, blue, indigo, and violet.

The ancient Egyptians and Babylonians wore amulets of certain colors to bless their wearers with the favour of their gods and to bring them into daily contact with divine beings. Color was used to bring success in commerce; to prevent disease; to afford safety from shipwreck, lightning, and animal attacks; to assure abundant harvests; and to control the elements.

The philosopher Empedocles named white, black, red, and yellow-ochre and associated them with the four elements. However, the only associations of his that we are certain of today are white with fire and black with water.

Aristotle, in the fourth century BCE, considered blue and yellow to be the true primary colors and related them to life's polarities: Sun and Moon, male and female, stimulus and sedation, expansion and contraction, out and in. He also associated colors with the four elements of fire, earth, air, and water. His principles were applied for two thousand years, until Isaac Newton's discoveries relating to the refraction of light, in the seventeenth and eighteenth centuries, replaced them in general color theory.

Hippocrates, the father of medicine, used color extensively in medicine and recognized that the therapeutic effects of a white violet would be quite different from those of a purple one. Avicenna, in the eleventh century, believed that a person's physical coloring indicated their predisposition to various diseases and always took account of the patients coloring in diagnosis. In the fifteenth century, Paracelsus placed particular importance on the role of color in healing.

Modern color theory harks back to the work of Aristotle. Links have been developed between patterns of color and personality types. Using Aristotle's idea that blue and yellow are the true primary colors, colors have been classified into cool and warm, then subdivided in terms of levels of intensity and the addition of black, white, or gray. This produces four tonal families associated with four personality types (as defined in Carl Jung's psychology), connecting yellow with extroversion and blue with introversion.

Color therapists believe that color can stimulate your resources on several levels – mental, emotional, and spiritual – and improve your health. Therefore, the choice of color is an integral part of making an amulet.

Colors can be incorporated into your amulet in a variety of ways. For example, when making paper amulets you can dye the paper with food dyes or use colored ink. Depending on what your purpose is, you may want to use more than one color. A combination can be used to achieve the exact balance of vibrations that you want.

In the past, the color chosen for a particular type of amulet depended on its astrological associations. The color chosen was one that corresponded with the planet under whose auspices the talisman was prepared. However, other associations are also made with colors and these can be used when making your amulet.

Traditionally, color has always been important in magic. Magician's writings were usually in red ink. Color was a potent force in resisting evil and overthrowing demons.

Amulets were traditionally red, blue, yellow, green, and white. Red stones tended to be used for the treatment of disease and to protect from fire and lightning. Blue and violet stones were associated with virtue and faith. They were hung about the necks of children to assure the watchfulness of heaven and to make them obedient to their parents. Yellow stones represented happiness and prosperity. Green stones were connected with fertility. White stones averted the evil eye.

If you make your amulet with parchment paper, the color of your ink should correspond with the planet associated with that amulet. Alternatively, you can buy or dye paper to the correct color. When you use a gem or stone to make an amulet, you will find that the meaning of that particular stone is related to its color.

Colors may also be related to the chakras as each chakra has its own color. The use of color can help to bring you back into balance. Using the chakra system, a color vibration travels, via the nervous system, to the part of the body that needs it.

Astrology and Color

Using astrological principles is a traditional way to choose a color for your amulet. If you want to restrain someone who has a prominent Mars in their birth chart, the gems colors and metals relating to Saturn can be chosen. If you want to help someone who is moody and taciturn – Saturn qualities – you can use the gems, colors, and metals of Mars. To use color in this way requires knowledge of both the qualities and colors associated with each of the planets.

Modern astrology tends to associate colors with the zodiac signs, whereas traditionally the strongest associations were made between colors and planets. There are various combinations of colors relating to the planets depending on your source. However, there are generally accepted correspondences that you can use without further study.

In astrology, colors can be used in two ways – as transmitters of influences and to signify a person or object. In the first case, color is used for its effect in the same way as a color therapist, interior designer, or magician uses red to produce a sense energy and warmth. In the second case, the planet is interpreted as referring to an object or person characterized by the color. For instance, the planet Mars refers to a person characterized by red.

Medieval astrologers extensively used lists of colors to indicate clothing and objects. These lists are based on a much older tradition. As they are based on the impressions that the items would make, there are many overlaps, the choice often depending on shade and texture. For example, Marsilio Ficino suggested that rich shades of purple are associated with Jupiter and the Sun; pale ones with Venus and the Moon. Practical considerations are also involved. Blue was listed infrequently, as good quality blue dye was expensive. New lists appeared with each new generation and modern astrologers have continued to devise them.

Planetary Associations

Sun – Gold, yellow or orange. Some older sources also suggest red (scarlet) and purple.

Moon – Silver or white. A range of other colors has been associated with the Moon including orange/yellow, blue, and green.

Mercury – Mixed colors. In addition, blue, gray, violet, and pink have been associated with Mercury. The tendency is to associate any mixed colors with Mercury.

Venus – Green, especially light green. Light blue, bluish green, white, and pastel colors in general are often associated with Venus.

Mars – Red. This is consistent in all sources. Occasionally bright yellow has been associated with Mars.

Jupiter – Purple or blue. Dark green and brown have also been associated with Jupiter.

Saturn – Black. Very dark colors such as dark brown are also associated with Saturn.

The modern planets were discovered long after these associations were made, but some authorities have associated them with colors.

Uranus – Turquoise and sometimes emerald green, mixed colors, metallic hues.

Neptune – Sea green, as Pisces.

Pluto – Black and as Saturn.

Zodiac signs

The colors relating to the zodiac signs are derived from the planets that rule each sign. Again, there are a variety of correspondences, although some combinations are more accepted than others. In terms of making amulets, these associations are likely to be less important unless detailed astrological work is being undertaken. However, some people choose to relate the Sun sign of the amulet wearer to the amulet.

Aries – Red (bright colors, yellow, white, pink). Ruled by Mars.

Taurus – Green (brown, yellow, white, light blue, earth colors). Ruled by Venus.

Gemini –Yellow/green (mixed, white, red, light/sky blue). Ruled by Mercury.

Cancer –White or gray (green, brown, blue/gray). Ruled by the Moon.

Leo – Gold or yellow (brown, red, green, orange). Ruled by the Sun.

Virgo –White (lilac, crimson, white, yellow, purple, green). Ruled by Mercury.

Libra –Pink or blue/green (gray, green, black/brown, red, all pastels). Ruled by Venus.

Scorpio – Black (dark red, deep orange, strong contrasting hues, gray, yellow, green, purple). Ruled by Mars traditionally, by Pluto in modern astrology.

Sagittarius – Purple or dark blue (red, gray, yellow, yellow/green). Ruled by Jupiter.

Capricorn – Black (greenish blue, white, brown, deep earth colors). Ruled by Saturn.

Aquarius – Green (yellow, gray, blue, mixed colors, metallic and electric colors.) Ruled by Saturn traditionally, by Uranus in modern astrology.

Pisces – Violet, blue/gray, olive (green, white, dull yellows.) Ruled by Jupiter traditionally, by Neptune in modern astrology.

Colors and Their Associations and Meanings

Red

Red is the color of blood, birth, and death. It is related to the planet Mars and the element fire.

In ancient times, red stones were worn as antidotes to poison, to keep your thoughts pure, and to banish anger and violent emotions. Red was also used as a guard against fire and lightning. In ancient Egypt, red symbolized masculinity, life, warmth, and danger. It was the opposite of the feminine white. In Egyptian art, women are white and the men brown (which was considered a shade of red). The goddess Isis is often represented by a serpent, and red is a color peculiar to her. Ancient Egyptian amulets made of red jasper, red faïence, and red glass were worn by soldiers and men whose work or duties brought them into conflict with their enemies, to prevent them from being wounded, or if wounded, to stop the flow of blood. Red amulets were also worn by women to prevent bleeding.

Traditionally, anyone who finds a red ribbon, tape, or anything red, especially if it is wool, will have luck in love. It must be picked up and carried as an amulet – when the finder picks it up from the ground, he or she must make a wish for the love of some person, or for luck in love.

Red is commonly found in ancient medicine. Scarlet cloth has been used for many centuries to stop bleeding. It has also been used against smallpox. Sometimes, physicians would prescribe red medicines and foods so that everything the patient ate or saw was crimson. English physicians once wore scarlet cloaks as a distinguishing mark of their profession. In rural Massachusetts, a red flag was displayed to call the doctor as he made his rounds. In Ireland and Russia, red flannel was a remedy for scarlet fever. Red wool was applied to relieve sprains in Scotland, sore throat in Ireland, and to prevent fevers in Macedonia. Red thread was thought necessary in the teething of English children.

The breath of a red ox was used against convulsions. Red sealing wax was used for eruptions and red coral kept teeth from loosening in England and relieved head troubles in Portugal. Red was used to overcome nightmares in Japan. In Macedonia, red yarn was tied on the bedroom door after the birth of a child to bind evil. In China, the ruby was worn to promote long life and a ribbon of red cloth was tied to the child's pigtail for the same reason. In India and Persia, a garnet was used in the same way. Roman coral and red carnelian drove away the evils of disease.

Red has the longest wavelength and is a powerful color. Although it isn't technically the most visible, it has the property of appearing to be nearer than it is and therefore it grabs our attention first. This is why it is used for warnings and in traffic lights. Pure red is the simplest color, with no subtlety. It is stimulating and lively.

Red is used to promote courage and lend energy to the body. Red is active, daring, passionate, and optimistic. It enhances alertness and encourages activity. Those languages, which only have words for three basic colors, always select black, white, and red. It represents physical courage, strength, warmth, energy, basic survival, sexuality, stimulation, masculinity, and excitement. Negatively it is associated with anger, defiance, being demanding, aggression, visual impact (as used in danger signs), and strain. It is used to bring vitality and movement and is primarily a stimulating energy.

Red is used to increase energy, improve circulation and protect against arthritis and all blood disorders. It is used to loosen, open up, and release stiffness and constrictions.

Pink

Pink is a receptive color and is ruled by the planet Venus. It is often used to attract love or to strengthen love already present. It can also be worn to promote self-love.

Being a tint of red, pink also affects us physically, but soothes, rather than stimulates. Red is the only color that has an entirely separate name for its tint. For example, tints of blue and green are simply called light blue and light green. Pink is a powerful color, psychologically. It represents the feminine principle, and survival of the species.

Pink helps to promote peace, happiness, joy, and laughter. It symbolizes love, friendship, relationships, family, and interchanges and stimulates the lighter emotions, attracting friends and encouraging openness towards others.

Yellow

Yellow is the color of the workings of the conscious mind. It aids logical thinking and enhances memory, writing, speech, and study. Yellow is ruled by the Sun and associated with the element of air.

Like the color of gold, yellow represents the highest of the physical colors. In ancient Egypt, amongst other places, yellow was seen to represent the Sun. "Worth its weight in gold" applies to yellow.

Yellow was used to cure jaundice because of the yellowing of skin caused by the disease. In Germany, jaundice disease was attacked with yellow turnips, gold coins, saffron, and many other yellow items. The English used yellow spiders as a remedy. In Greece, an affliction called "gold disease" was treated by drinking wine in which a gold piece had been placed and was then exposed to the stars for three nights. Bits of gold were also sprinkled on food as a safeguard against poisoning. In Malaysia, disease and plague were driven away in a yellow ship.

Yellow is used to produce detachment and reduce depression. It is seen as the most positive of colors, the opposite of blue, and the closest to pure light. As a projective color, yellow symbolizes protection, attraction, persuasion, confidence, and communication. It is related to movement and exchange. Yellow is a good color to use when you want to increase your personal power.

Yellow has a relatively long wavelength, and is emotionally stimulating. It can lift spirits and self-esteem, and aid in building confidence and optimism.

The blend of yellow with other colors relates to a particular form of intellectual prowess. Combined with red to make orange, it corresponds to earthly and mundane affairs; combined with blue to make green, it indicates subjectivity and inspiration.

Yellow helps strengthen the nerves and enriches the mind and brain. It helps awaken mental inspiration and stimulates higher mentality. It is the main color for nervous or nerve related conditions.

Yellow can be used for conditions of the stomach, liver, and intestines. It helps the pores of the skin and aids scarred tissue in healing itself. It is also used to remove toxins from the system and against parasites.

Orange

The color orange is often used to symbolize the Sun. Orange is more ambitious and self-sufficient than red, and lacks its warmth. It is used to bring joy and heal grief.

As a combination of red and yellow, orange is stimulating and focuses our minds on issues of physical comfort. It is used to protect and promote illumination and is related to personal power.

Orange also boosts low self-esteem, because it expands the awareness of self-worth. It is thought to be luck-attracting and a symbol of success, worn to assure a positive outcome. Orange helps assimilate new ideas and stimulate mental enlightenment.

Orange is used against fear, depression, or lack of energy. Medically it is used to combat arthritis and gallstones and as a mild painkiller.

Green

Green is a healing and fertile color. It is related to the planet Venus. In ancient Egypt, green symbolized life, growth, and rebirth; it was opposed to black, the color of death. It has always been known as a healing color. The ancient Egyptians and Chinese used green in this way.

Green lies in the center of the spectrum, so it is a color of balance. It is healing, sympathetic, steadfast, and restrained. Green can be used to reduce stress and movement, and is a soothing color.

Green is the color of nature, fertility, and life. It has often been linked with red in religion and magic. Green symbolizes money, luck, and prosperity. It can be worn to safeguard health.

Green is calming and can be used to calm babies. It is also used for heart problems, and to combats muscle spasms. Green is believed to affect blood pressure and all conditions of the heart.

Green corresponds to growth and creativity and is a natural harmonizer.

Black

Black is formal, conventional, and dignified. In ancient Egypt, it symbolized night, death, and magic, and was seen as the opposite of green, the color of life. Black is the color of death and brings forward images of darkness. It is ruled by the planet Saturn.

The Greeks believed that a raven's eggs would restore blackness to the hair. The eggs were thought to be so effective that a Greek man would keep his mouth filled with oil when treating his hair to keep his teeth from turning black. Black threads from the wool of black sheep cured earache in Ireland, England, and parts of Vermont. Black snails were rubbed on warts.

In France, the skins of black animals were applied warm to the limbs to relieve rheumatism. It was believed that a black fowl, if buried where caught, would cure epilepsy. The blood of a black cat has been prescribed for pneumonia in England and South Africa.

Technically, black is not a color. It is an absence of color and what the eye perceives when all light has been absorbed and none reflected. Black is the image of lifelessness. This means that it can be a good color to wear when you want to feel anonymous and safe.

Black symbolizes self-control, resilience, and quiet power. It is a protective and grounding color. As it is the absence of color and light, it has been traditionally used for negative purposes. Although sometimes used to represent bad habits and disease within magic, black is not a good color for amulets except when an effect particular to Saturn is strongly desired.

Black can create protective barriers, and absorb the energy coming toward you.

White

In ancient Egypt, white symbolized purity and femininity, contrasting with the masculine red. It is associated with the Moon.

As black is total absorption, white is total reflection. It reflects the full force of the spectrum into our eyes. White is purity and uncompromising, it is clean, hygienic, and sterile. White represents fate, purity, truth, and sincerity. Plutarch mentioned that a white reed found on the banks of a river while one journeyed to sacrifice at dawn, if strewn in a wife's bedroom, drove an adulterer mad and forced him to confess his sin. White is linked with sleep and considered a lucky color, used to promote good fortune. It is believed that white contains all colors, and can be magically charged to act as protection. White represents the awakened spirit, perfection and the light of the Christ and Buddhic consciousness. White can be strengthening and help to clarify the mind.

Blue

Blue is idealistic, rational, honest, and tranquil and is associated with the element of water. Many languages do not distinguish between blue and green. In ancient Egypt, light blue was considered green and dark blue, black. Light blue is more spiritual, dark blue more sociable.

Blue and green have been used mostly as preventives, to ward off the evil eye, and spare the wearer from demons. In Ireland, blue ribbon was used for the croup, and indigestion was relieved when a person measured their waist with a green thread in the name of the Trinity and then ate three dandelion leaves on a piece of bread and butter for three consecutive mornings.

Blue objects do not appear to be as close to us as red ones. Research has shown many times that blue is the world's favourite color, even though it can be perceived as cold, unemotional and unfriendly. Blue is usually seen as a color of the mind and soothing. Strong blues will stimulate clear thought and lighter blues will calm the mind and aid concentration.

Blue is also the color of spiritual power, intuition, psychic faculties, and the subjective mind. Light or bright blue is the tone best used for positive results. Light blue is symbolic of understanding, tranquility, and spiritual awareness whereas dark blue is symbolic of introspection, spiritual values, wisdom, and healing

In healing, blue is used to soothe pain, fevers, and inflammation as well as for treating shock. It is also used to help bleeding and cure sore throats. Blue can have a sedative effect.

Purple

Purple is associated with the planet Jupiter. It is the color of royalty and gives dignity and authority.

Purple symbolizes ambition and will power, and has long been associated with mysticism and purification. It is powerful when worn during meditation and psychic work. Purple is a color of healing and peace and is associated with organized religion.

Purple is used to strengthen the immune and nervous system and to combat stress and fatigue. Indigo is a purifier of the bloodstream and used to heal mental problems. It is also used in dealing with ailments of the eyes and ears.

Violet is the shortest wavelength and relates to a higher level of thought. It is generally not used for physical conditions but instead for spiritually related problems. It stimulates deep mental activity.

Brown

Brown is a warm neutral color and in many languages is identified with red. It is practical, earthy, obstinate, and conscientious.

Brown usually consists of red and yellow, with a large percentage of black and so has much of the same seriousness as black, but is warmer and softer. Brown is associated with the earth and the natural world. It is a solid, reliable, and supportive color.

Brown can indicate practicality and symbolize growth or the desire for accomplishment. Darker browns can help ground (bring down to earth) intentions and actions but can also cause stagnation and slowness.

CHAPTER 7

MAGIC SQUARES

Magic squares are extremely old and have been used in many different cultures. About three thousand years ago, they appeared in China, and later in India and Iraq. It's believed that in China there were two traditions. One was based on the I Ching and the other reached Mesopotamia via India.

Legend says that Adam invented the square. The square has been used for a variety of purposes, against stomach pains, to render yourself invisible, to protect from the evil eye, and to open locks.

The first Chinese magic square is seen in the scroll of the river Lo – the Lo-Shu, a scroll believed to have been created by Fuh-Hi, the mythical founder of Chinese civilization, who lived from 2858 to 2738 BCE.

The scroll is a 3 x 3 (9-grid) magic square, where odd numbers are expressed as white dots, or yang symbols, and even numbers are expressed as black dots, or yin symbols. The odd numbers are symbols of heaven, while even numbers are symbols of the earth. The first appearance of the Lo-Shu was in writings from between the latter part of the Chou dynasty (951-1126 CE) and the beginning of the Southern Sung dynasty (1127-1133 CE).

In ancient Egypt, magic squares were used to represent the difference between order and chaos. Squares made up of two or four cells represented chaos because they were incapable of forming magic squares. Magic squares 3 x 3 or larger were dedicated to the Sun, Moon, and planets in the form of amulets and talismans. These were made by taking a magic square and placing it in a polygon with the number of sides of the polygon equal to the root of the square. In other words a 3 x 3 magic square was placed in a triangle, a 5 x 5 was placed in a pentagon. These polygons were then placed in a circle, and in between the sides of the polygon and the circle were inscribed signs of the zodiac. Then the name of the corresponding planet was added.

Little is known of magic squares in ancient India. It has been suggested that magic squares have Indian roots, since they are commonly worn as amulets and talismans and can be found in the architecture of that country. In India, magic squares are often written on a white porcelain plate, or on paper. The inscription is then washed off with water and the latter drunk. Magic squares are also carried on the person or are burnt, so that the individual is smoked with their fumes. They are also often engraved on rings.

Magic squares were introduced into Europe in the fifteenth century and became very popular through the writings of such people as Heinrich Cornelius Agrippa.

The squares were never just mathematical games, but were regarded as magical and they have been linked with astrology since their beginning. They were assigned into planetary categories based on their uses and the purpose of sigils that had been derived from their patterns.

A magic square is a square in which all the rows add up to the same sum. For example:

4	3	8
9	5	1
2	7	6

In this square each row or diagonal adds up to 15.

The numbers in a magic square are usually consecutive integers. There are two types of magic squares – odd and even. An odd magic square is one where the number of cells on each side of the square is odd. In all magic squares, the sum of each row and each column should equal the same amount. Odd magic squares have additional properties in that the sum of each main diagonal should equal the same amount as the sum of each row and column, and the sum of any two numbers geometrically equidistant from the center should be twice the amount of the center number. Even magic squares have the additional property that the sum of any two numbers geometrically equidistant from the center should equal the sum of the first and last numbers in the series of numbers you are working with.

There is more than one combination of each set of numbers that fit the criteria of a magic square or *kamea*. Some squares have another distinguishing characteristic. Following the numbers in their natural order produces a symmetrical pattern which gives us what is called the kameic path or kameic. This is the key to the energies that the kamea can channel.

However, not all mathematical magic squares are symmetrical. Some modern books give squares that don't show a symmetrical property. This is often because a better-known mathematical magic square is substituted. A successful sigil or talisman can still be made using these squares, but it will not be as powerful.

Magic squares were often inscribed onto amulets as protectors. The 72 square, as shown below, was used in this way. You would write the name of your enemy below the square and wear it so that he would be powerless against you.

28	35	2	7
6	3	32	31
34	29	8	1
4	5	30	33

Planetary Associations

Certain squares are linked with planets. These associations come from the Babylonians. The concept is based on their belief that the smallest planet is the farthest away from earth and the largest the closest. The smallest planet gets the smallest square, so we arrive at the following order:

Saturn – square of 3

Jupiter – square of 4

Mars – square of 5

Sun – square of 6

Venus – square of 7

Mercury – square of 8

Moon – square of 9

This applies to the simplest squares possible, those with the lowest numbers.

Each planet is linked to a particular kamea square. Each of these squares has a *seal* which is the geometric pattern created by following the numbers in the order of their value. This pattern touches upon all the numbers of the square. This seal is used to represent the entire square. There is also an *intelligence* and a *spirit* associated with each kamea, derived from the key numbers of the square using a Hebrew form of numerology. The intelligence is viewed as a guiding, inspiring, or informing entity. The spirit is traditionally considered more of a neutral force. Each intelligence and spirit has a sigil, which is a glyph of the associated name, number, and force. These sigils are made by converting the name of the spirit or intelligence to a numerical form based on Hebrew letter values and the Kabbalah. There is more about sigils in the following chapter.

As well as being associated with the seven planets, each kamea is linked with a planetary Sephirah on the Tree of Life. The number of divisions in a row or column of the magic square is governed by the number of the appropriate Sephirah.

Number	Sephirah	Planet
3	Binah	Saturn
4	Chesed	Jupiter

5	Geburah	Mars
6	Tiphareth	Sun
7	Netzach	Venus
8	Hod	Mercury
9	Yesod	Moon

Saturn Square

Whatever sequence of numbers you use to add up to ten, five will be the arithmetic mean. Therefore, five was considered the number of justice.

4	9	2
3	5	7
8	1	6

This particular square is extremely common in many ancient philosophies. It can be found in the Kabbalah, Tibetan astrology, I Ching, Pythagorean writings, and many occult, alchemic, and magical traditions.

Using numerology, the number 15 adds up to 6 (i.e. 1+5) resulting in 666 on all sides. Six we know represents the Celestial Star of the Macrocosm and the Star of David. 6+6+6 = 18 which reduces to 9. The square itself has 9 boxes. The 9 ties this square to the 9th chamber of the Kabbalah, which is also called the Square of Saturn. As it has 3 divisions or boxes on each side, Saturn is attributed to Binah (the third Sephirah of the Tree of Life).

One of the most well-known and ancient 3 x 3 squares can be found in the I Ching. The legend is that a turtle crawled out of the Lo River with this square imprinted on its shell. It is called Lo Shu. The Tibetan system of astrology utilizes all 9 permutations of the Saturn Square called Mewas. They are associated with the calendar. The Saturn Square is situated at the center. This is based on the astrology of the elements, which originated in

China and is highly developed in both Tibetan and Chinese astrology. Each Mewa is associated with a color related to each of the five elements. The center square represents the Earth element. The Saturn square is commonly found at the center of many Tibetan paintings. The system of the Mewas is dynamic, they move with each month, day, and year. The course of movement within each square describes a diagram similar to the seal of Saturn used in Western magic.

Practitioners of Kabbalah are intrigued by the 3 x 3 magic square because the sum of each row, column, and diagonal is 15, the same as the numerical value of Y-H, the first two letters of God's name in Hebrew, transliterated into our alphabet – YHWH.

The Saturn square gives the opportunity to attain worldly success. It is also believed to be helpful in curing depression. Sometimes inscribed on lead, it helps with childbirth and can add strength to an amulet for protection or safety. It is painted in white on a black background.

Jupiter Square

1	15	14	4
12	6	7	9
8	10	11	5
13	3	2	16

The Jupiter square can be made from any metal or paper and is often engraved on tin or coral. It should be drawn on a Tuesday. It gives the wearer power, prestige, and authority. It can add a *jovial* atmosphere to an event and be used as a cure for depression. It helps with prosperity, favor, love, peace, and concord and in appeasing enemies. It is painted in orange-bronze on a blue background.

Mars Square

11	24	7	20	3
4	12	25	8	16
17	5	13	21	9
10	18	1	14	22
23	6	19	2	15

The Mars square is often written on a copper plate and should be inscribed on a Tuesday. It protects the wearer from accidents and injury and increases strength in combat and conflict. It is painted in green on a red background.

Sun Squares

The magic square of the Sun, was extremely important in antiquity because of all the symbolism it possessed involving the perfect number 6. There are six sides to a cube. The numbers 1, 2, and 3, when added or multiplied together, are equal to 6, and the sum of all the numbers from 1 to 36 arranged in a 6 x 6 magic square are equal to the number 666. The sum of any row, column, or diagonal is equal to the number 111. In the Roman Empire, possessing a Sun magic square could get you burned at the stake. The Sun square has also been associated with Jesus.

The Sun square is used to give peace of mind. In India, it is often engraved on copper or stainless steel and worn around the neck. It can be drawn on paper and carried in a purse or in a pocket. The best time to construct it is on a Sunday, the day of the Sun. It can be transcribed on gold and is used to bring glory or power. It can also influence your friendship

with those in charge. It can be wrapped in yellow silk to enhance its powers. It is painted in purple or magenta on a yellow background.

1	35	34	3	32	6
30	8	28	27	11	7
24	23	15	16	14	19
13	17	21	22	20	18
12	26	9	10	29	25
31	2	4	33	5	36

Venus Square

22	47	16	41	10	35	4
5	23	48	17	42	11	29
30	8	24	49	18	36	12
12	21	7	25	43	19	37
38	14	32	1	26	44	20
21	39	8	33	2	27	45
31	15	40	9	34	3	28

The Venus square enhances peace of mind and makes you more attractive
to the opposite sex. It should be constructed on a Friday and can be made

of any material. It makes peace, attracts women, is used for conception, and provides luck for travel. It is painted in yellow on a dark green background.

Mercury Square

8	58	59	5	4	62	63	1
49	15	14	52	53	11	10	56
41	23	22	44	48	19	18	45
32	34	38	29	25	35	39	28
40	26	27	37	36	30	31	33
17	47	46	20	21	43	42	24
9	55	51	12	13	54	50	16
64	2	3	61	60	6	7	57

The Mercury square can be engraved on a silver plate or drawn on paper on a Wednesday. It protects from enemies and increases memory retention. Mercury squares can also be used to enhance divinatory abilities and perception. It is painted blue on an orange-bronze background.

Moon Square
The Moon square can be engraved on silver or written on white paper. It is used to give good friends and respect in the community and should be drawn on a Monday. The Moon square also offers safety in travel, increased wealth, and health, and drives away enemies. It is painted in yellow on a purple or magenta background.

37	78	29	70	21	62	13	54	5
6	38	79	30	71	22	63	14	46
47	7	39	60	31	72	23	55	15
16	48	8	40	91	32	64	24	56
57	17	49	9	41	73	33	65	25
26	58	18	50	1	42	74	34	66
67	27	59	10	51	2	43	75	35
38	68	19	60	11	52	3	44	76
77	28	69	20	61	12	53	4	45

Alphamagic Squares

Only one magic square that relies on letters rather than numbers has survived from antiquity. This is the *SATOR* square.

S	A	T	O	R
A	R	E	P	O
T	E	N	E	T
O	P	E	R	A
R	O	T	A	S

The five Latin words appear in the same order horizontally and vertically, and the five rows can be read palindromically. They also form a sentence "Arepo, the sower, guides the wheels at work." This has also been translated as "The sower Arepo leads with his hand (work) the plough (wheels)."

The square originally appeared in a different form and was reversed at an unknown date.

```
R O T A S
O P E R A
T E N E T
A R E P O
S A T O R
```

It is often believed to have a Christian significance, because it contains, jumbled up, the words *"pater noster"* (our father) in the form of a cross, along with the letters "a" and "o", which are the Greek letters Alpha and Omega, used of God, for example, in Revelations.

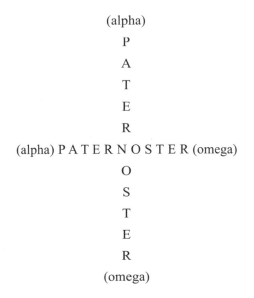

```
                    (alpha)
                       P
                       A
                       T
                       E
                       R
(alpha) P A T E R N O S T E R (omega)
                       O
                       S
                       T
                       E
                       R
                    (omega)
```

The conventional academic view was that this letter square had been a secret sign of recognition among early Christians, but this view changed when it was discovered among the ruins of Pompeii. Some authorities believe it to be Mithraic in origin. It is possible that although it may not be

Christian in origin, the square was adopted by some believers.

In occult literature, the square is depicted as the Second Pentacle of Saturn, adding up to the numerical value of the Tetragrammaton. However, although there is much speculation, its meaning remains unknown.

The SATOR square has been fashioned into amulets. In medieval times, it was used as protection against sorcery, poisonous air, colic, pestilence, and for protecting cow's milk.

Making a Magic Square Amulet

The simplest way to make a magic square amulet is to take a piece of good quality paper – you want it to last – and inscribe the square you want on the day (and preferable the hour) ruled by the relevant planet. If you choose to have it inscribed on metal, you should use the metal appropriate to the planet.

CHAPTER 8

SIGNS AND SIGILS

The word *sigil* comes from the Latin *sigillum*, meaning sign, or signature. It usually denotes a magical sigil, or a glyph used in ritual or sympathetic magic as a focus, or for summoning angels, demons, or spirits. It is derived from a name, word, or magical formula by an analogical process. If the process is reversed, then the name or word may be retrieved from the pattern of the sigil. Sigils as the signature of a spirit began in antiquity and reached a peak of popularity during the Renaissance.

The use of sigils in magical practice is ancient. In early history, symbols were used as languages and codes. This can be seen in the history of Ancient Egypt and their hieroglyphics.

Sigils can represent complex concepts. The pentacle is the most powerful sigil used in witchcraft and by many occultists. Other sigils serve to identify organizations. Individuals can adopt their personal sigils. They have a personal, secret meaning and are often inscribed on magical tools. Sigils also serve as amulets, talismans, or meditation tools.

Sigil designs are derived from geometric shapes, astrological signs, or symbols used in alchemy. Some sigils are attained through intuition and inspiration. Many come through meditation and scrying, when a certain pattern seems to appear upon the object that the individual is gazing at. The most powerful sigils are those that you create yourself. The glyphs are used as a way to bridge the gap between the conscious and subconscious mind.

How Sigils Work

There is no power inherent in any set of symbols; it's the subconscious manipulation of the symbols that makes them magical. Conscious awareness is the state of mind that receives direct input from the senses and processes them. Subconscious awareness is the type that lies deep inside the mind and is usually unreachable through direct connection by conscious awareness. It controls dreams and maintains the highly complex functions of the human body. The conscious mind isn't capable of performing magic, so the subconscious mind must have the magical intent implanted in it so that it can unconsciously manipulate information to bring about the result.

The conscious awareness is where our known desires are located. Magical work takes place in our subconscious awareness. There is no way to directly transfer conscious desires to the subconscious. Because they can't have direct connections, we need to trick the subconscious awareness into accepting conscious thoughts. Your subconscious mind requires symbolism created by the conscious mind to motivate it to accomplish your desires. A sigil has meaning to your conscious mind – and can be sent to your subconscious to will it to achieve your desire. A sigil created by anyone other than you will not have the same powers or be as effective for you as a sigil you make yourself.

How to Make a Sigil

There are many different ways to create a sigil. The guidelines given here will help you to get started, so that eventually you can evolve your own sigil-making method. No special tools or equipment are needed beyond a pencil and paper, and even these aren't always necessary.

One of the methods of devising sigils is to trace the desired word over magic squares, or tables of letters or numbers, to reveal a symbol. A sigil should be drawn when you are in a meditative state or focusing on your intended goal.

In magical practice, sigils are drawn and then destroyed to bring about the desired effect. They can be traced in air, carved on candles, or drawn on paper and burned. However, sigils are also commonly used for amulets and talismans.

The first step is to write down your conscious desire. You need to be specific and use words that are geared towards making something happen. If you are want to make a sigil to help you find a better job, your desire should be something along the lines of, "I will find a better job" rather than "I want a better job." The more specific and forceful you are, the more chance you have of manifesting that desire.

Once your statement is written down, rearrange the letters and then randomly or systematically remove certain ones. There are numerous ways of doing this. The letters can be converted to numbers, run into a formula, and then turned back into letters. Or you can just remove letters that appear more than once. At this point, your sigil creation will take one of two paths.

The first path is graphical. Now that you have your mixed up letters, you should draw a picture or symbol using those letters. Make sure that you use every single letter. You can bend them, stretch them, squeeze them, and contort them in any way you choose. The letters can be linked to each other, or superimposed on top of each other, in any way you want.

Once you have your symbol containing all of your letters, you simplify it. You can slide the lines around a little or remove certain ones. Continue to play with the symbol and redraw it until you have found your sigil. All that is important is that you know what it means. No one else needs to be able to recognize your intentions for these symbols so there is no right or wrong way of finalizing your design. Enclosing the image helps make it more concise – drawing a circle or similar shape around it is common practice.

A second method is to arrange the letters to form a mantra. Rearrange the letters to form something that flows smoothly when pronounced. If that is difficult, you can go back to the second step and instead of removing letters, double all of your vowels or adapt it similarly. What is important is that your end product is something you can remember and flows smoothly so that you will have no problem chanting it.

Another method of creating a graphic sigil is to draw a simple picture of the intent. For example, you could draw a little stick figure, with your initials on it, sitting behind the wheel of a car. The picture is then changed to alter it beyond recognition, and then treated as a glyph.

Once you have created your sigil, you can discard the piece of paper with the original sentence on it. From this point onward, the sigil isn't looked at as derivative of words, or a list of letters, but as a picture.

Charging or Consecrating your Sigil

The act of charging is particular to Western magic; many cultures don't bother with this step. Whether you do is entirely up to you. Every person has their own way of charging sigils. The concept behind it is that you have the sigil created, you have the desire erased from your conscious awareness, and you have the desire linked to the subconscious. Now you just have to start the subconscious. This is what you accomplish through charging the sigil.

One method is to chant the mantra sigil or visualize the graphical sigil as you meditate or while dancing or drumming. The idea is to open the gates of the deep mind and cause the sigil to be absorbed into it. This has the effect of the sigil charging you.

The Numerology of Sigils

You can convert your name to a numerical form and trace it on a magic square in order to make a personalised sigil in the aspect of that particular planet.

For example, Saturn rules worldly success. You could base your sigil on the Saturn square if you are seeking business success. This method uses Western, or Pythagorean, numerology. There is another system of numerology, called Chaldean, which is more commonly used in India. Each letter has a numerical equivalent assigned to it but the numbers are different according to the system your use. If you use numerology already, you will have chosen a system and should continue with that system. Otherwise, it's best to begin with the Pythagorean, although you may wish to experiment with both systems to see which works best for you. The number-letter equivalents are given for both systems in the table below.

Occasionally, you will get the same results in both systems.

Pythagorean

1	2	3	4	5	6	7	8	9
A	B	C	D	E	F	G	H	I
J	K	L	M	N	O	P	Q	R
S	T	U	V	W	X	Y	Z	

Chaldean

1	2	3	4	5	6	7	8
A	B	C	D	E	U	O	F
I	K	G	M	H	V	Z	P
J	R	L	T	N	W		
Q		S		X			
Y							

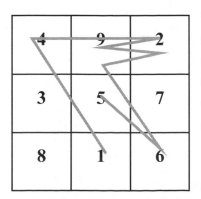

Take the key word relating to the thought behind your sigil. For example, if you are using a Saturn square to achieve your ambitions, your word could be "ambition." Find the numerical value of each letter in the word.

Under the Pythagorean system:

A= 1 M = 4 B = 2 I = 9 T = 2 I = 9
O = 6 N = 5

Take a copy of the Saturn square and starting with your first corresponding number and continuing through each in order, draw out your sigil.

This gives you the following sigil, representing your intention to achieve your ambitions.

You can then incorporate some of the other correspondences for Saturn to make your amulet more powerful, for example by drawing the sigil in black or by adding a Saturnine herb.

Each magic square has its own sigil similar to the one above and designed so as to touch all the numbers of the square. The seal is used in amulets to represent the square. There is also an intelligence and a spirit connected with each square, both of which are derived from the key numbers of the square. The intelligence of a planet is viewed as a guiding entity. The spirit of a planet is considered neutral. Each intelligence and spirit has a sigil. These are obtained by converting their name numerologically. These calculations are done using the numerical values of the Hebrew letters in the name. The traditional seals and sigils don't in all cases follow the entire numerical sequence of each name. Some have been shortened for easier use.

A table known as the Aiq Bekar (Kabbalah of the Nine Chambers) is used to place the Hebrew letters into nine boxes. For instance, A or *Aleph* has a value of 1 – see the upper right-hand chamber in the table below.

Sh	L	G	R	K	B	Q	Y	A
300	30	3	200	20	2	100	10	1
M	S	V	K	N	H	Th	M	D
600	60	6	500	50	5	400	40	4
Tz	Tz	T	P	P	Ch	N	O	Z
900	90	9	800	80	8	700	70	7

For example, when creating the sigil of Zazel, the spirit of Saturn, the numeric value of the Hebrew letters of the name (ZAZL in Hebrew) are converted into a series of numbers.

Z = 7
A = 1
Z = 7
L = 30
7 1 7 30

The numbers are then connected by lines. As the Square of Saturn doesn't contain the value 30, the number can be substituted with any other letter in its chamber. Looking at the table we can see that L can be converted into a 3. A letter should never be reduced further than necessary. The code is now 7 1 7 3 and the sigil can be produced by connecting the numbers.

There are other, more complex ways of using the Aiq Bekar to create sigils, which result in some of the shapes you see below.

Saturn Sigil

If you place this over the Saturn square, you will see this arrangement is very clear. A line following 1-2-3, a line through 4-5-6 and a line following 7-8-9. This gets more complex as the squares get more complex and the system is not always this simple. The Saturn square counts 45 in total (all digits added together), so the names of the Saturn intelligence and spirit have a number-value of 45. The intelligence is called *Agiel*, the spirit *Zazel*.

Agiel

Zazel

In some systems, repeated letters are used before creating the line drawing. This is usually necessary if you are using a phrase, rather than a single word.

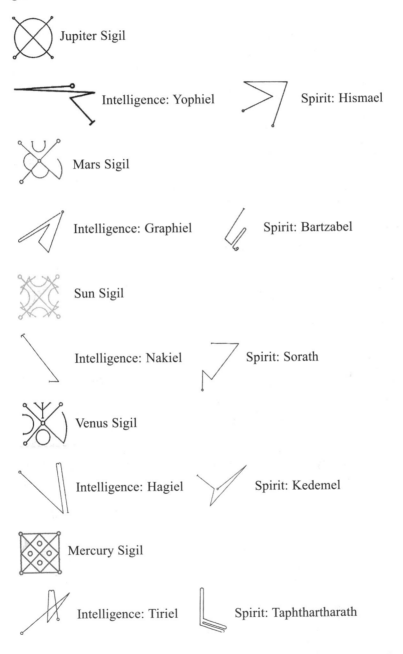

Jupiter Sigil

Intelligence: Yophiel

Spirit: Hismael

Mars Sigil

Intelligence: Graphiel

Spirit: Bartzabel

Sun Sigil

Intelligence: Nakiel

Spirit: Sorath

Venus Sigil

Intelligence: Hagiel

Spirit: Kedemel

Mercury Sigil

Intelligence: Tiriel

Spirit: Taphthartharath

 Moon Sigil

Other Sigils?

Intelligence of the intelligences Malcah Be-Tarshsim We-ad Ruachoth ha-chechalim

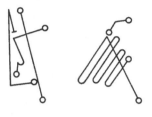

Spirit of the Spirits Sched Barschemoth Scharthan

Spirit: Chashmodai

The sigils for angels are often used in traditional magic to summon the spirit. There are also sigils associated with demons. The names of the angels seem to be traditional. Lists with names of fallen angels can be found in early writings such as the *Book of Enoch*. Angels are the beings that can transport messages to the right place in the heavenly court. Everything and everyone has an angel.

The planetary seals can be used to block that planet's energy. Blocking a planet's energy is useful when you intend to block the negative effects of a planet. To make use of this you need to have knowledge of astrology. One example of this type of use is when Mercury goes retrograde, or from our perception appears to be moving backwards in the heavens. It's possible to find out when this happens by consulting a book of tables of planetary positions, or an *ephemeris*. When Mercury is retrograde, there are problems in issues related to Mercury, particularly in communication. Mercury is retrograde about twenty per cent of the time. You can block the energy of Mercury by placing the planetary seal over the magic square of Mercury. However, you need to remember that when you do this, you are blocking all of the effects of a planet. The amulet is best made on the day of the week that corresponds to the planetary energy involved.

The table below gives some alternatives of planetary sigils dating from the seventeenth century. Some of these you will find more aesthetically pleasing than others, and if you're using them in combination with other images, some will be easy to incorporate in your final image.

Alternative Planetary Sigils

Saturn

Jupiter

Mars

Sun

Venus

Mercury

Moon

Angels related to each planet

⊟ ⅉ⸗ ⅁⅊   of Saturn

⅊ ⅉ ⅉ ♃   of Jupiter

ⅉ ⅉ ⅖ⅉ ⸗   of Mars

⅀ⅉ ⅉ ⅗ ☉   of the Sun

♉ ⌒⌒) ♀   of Venus

⊶⊕⊟⊶Ⅹ   of Mercury

ⅉ♭ ⊞♭ⅉⅿ⸗ ☾   of the Moon

CHAPTER 9

MAGIC WORDS

It was believed in the past that some words were so potent that nothing more was needed on an amulet. One phrase, the palindrome *ablanathanalba*, may have been the origin of *abracadabra*, which was rarely used before the Middle Ages. Another, *Aski Kataski*, was part of a longer magical formula known as *Ephesian letters*. The origin of these letters is unknown but, like other magic words, they were passed from culture to culture. Such letters were believed to have an inherent power apart from their meaning.

Abracadabra

Some amulets contain written charms, rather than symbols. One of the oldest, and most widely known, is the word *abracadabra*. The word is very ancient, and was first mentioned in a poem by Quintus Serenus Sammonicus in the second century CE. There are many theories about where it originated, but no-one knows for sure.

Sammonicus' poem was translated by the antiquarian John Aubrey, in the seventeenth century, as:

Abracadabra, strange mysterious word,
In order writ, can won'rous cures afford.
This be the rule:- a strip of parchment take,
Cut like a pyramid revers'd in make.
Abracadabra, first at length you name,
Line under line, repeating still the same:
Cut at its end, each line, one letter less,
Must then its predecessor line express;
'Till less'ning by degrees the charm descends

With conic form, and in a letter ends.
Round the sick neck the finish'd wonder tie,
And pale disease must from the patient fly.

Many people believe that abracadabra originated as a secret from a Gnostic sect in Alexandria called the Basilidians and was based on *Abrasax* (Abraxas), the name of their deity. It is also said to have been constructed from the initial letters of three Hebrew words, *Ab*, the father, *Ben*, the son, and *Acadsch*, the Holy Spirit. One hypothesis about the source of the word is Aramaic, *Avrah KaDabra,* which means "I will create as I speak" or from the Aramaic *abhadda kedhabhra*, meaning "disappear like this word." Rather than being used as a curse, the Aramaic phrase is believed to have been used as a means of treating illness. Another possible source is the Hebrew *Aberah KeDaber,* which also means "I will create as I speak" or the Hebrew *abreg ad Habra*, meaning "strike dead with thy lightning." Some have argued that the term may come from the Arabic *Abra Kadabra*, meaning "let the things be destroyed." It has also been claimed to come from Abracalan (or Aracalan), said to have been both a Syrian god and a Jewish magical symbol.

Abracadabra is a phrase that is universal in almost all languages. Because of its universality, it has been speculated that the word predates the confusion of languages granted at the Tower of Babel.

Written in the shape of a triangle on a piece of parchment and worn around the neck, the word was believed to have the power to cure toothaches, malaria and other diseases.

The usual form of abracadabra was:

```
ABRACADABRA
ABRACADABR
ABRACADAB
ABRACADA
ABRACAD
ABRACA
ABRAC
ABRA
ABR
AB
A
```

Sometimes, this occurs in slightly different arrangements, for example with the letters on the left in a straight, vertical line. By arranging the letters as shown above, the energies in the word are directed downwards. If written on parchment and hung around the neck, this arrangement acts as protection against evil spirits and the evil eye.

Ephesian Letters

The Ephesian letters probably had no special association with Ephesus. Ephesus was the capital of pro-consular Asia, located about halfway between Jerusalem and Rome, and was the approximate center of the Roman Empire. Founded about 1000 BCE, it was a busy port and called "The Treasure House of Asia." Ephesus was a meeting place of many currents of Hellenistic thought. It was famous for its charms, spells, and amulets. The letters are the "scrolls" referred to in Acts 19:19.

In their usual order, the letters are: *askion, kataskion, lix, tetrax, damnameneus* and *aision* (or *aisia*), though they can be rearranged. These words resemble but are not Greek words. They were in circulation since at least the fifth century BCE, though the first mention of them is a first century CE text apparently giving thanks for vengeance. Commonly used in curses, they also had protective qualities and were used to ward off spells. Before 300 CE, they were considered unintelligible to mortals, and therefore powerful.

Ablanathanalba

This is a Gnostic charm triangle, similar to the Abracadabra triangle and used for protection against evil forces. It was traditionally written on parchment, using special ink obtained from the acorn of a valonia oak tree.

```
A B L A N A T H A N A L B A
B L A N A T H A N A L B
L A N A T H A N A L
A N A T H A N A
N A T H A N
A T H A
T H
```

It is thought to be derived from the Hebrew, meaning "Thou art our father."

Abraxas

The sacred name Abraxas was inscribed on innumerable Gnostic gems. A great many explanations have been offered as to the origin and significance of the figure of the Abrasax god. It appears to have been invented by Basilides, chief of the Gnostic sect bearing his name, which flourished in the early part of the second century CE.

Abraxas is a Gnostic solar deity associated with Yahweh, Mithras and the Celtic Belenus, as well as Yeshu (Jesus). Amulets and seals bearing the figure of Abraxas were common in the second century, and were used as recently as the thirteenth century in the seals of the Knights Templar. By the Middle Ages, Abraxas was relegated to the ranks of demons.

The image most associated with Abraxas is a creature with the head of a rooster, the body of a man, and legs made of serpents or scorpions. He carries a whip and shield, called wisdom and power. Sometimes, he is depicted driving a chariot drawn by four horses, probably representing the elements.

The letters in Abraxas add up to 365, the number of days in a solar year, and the number of Aeons, or emanations, in Gnostic cosmology. Each of the seven letters represents one of the seven planets.

Abraxas gems are engraved with this word, either alone or with other names of God, and in connection with mystic figures and groups of letters. The magic word *ablanathanalba* also occurs alongside Abraxas.

Characteres

In the second century CE, a magical alphabet started circulating called the *characteres*. They were often used in curses. The letters of the alphabet were themselves magically effective, with the seven vowels thought to hold power, and associated with planets, angels, and sounds. Often, the Greek and Latin alphabet would be combined.

Magical Squares and Triangles

Magic words would often be arranged into squares, triangles, or diamonds, and palindromes were also quite common.

Charms

A charm is a verbal formula, spoken or written, to protect or heal. The words of the charm may command invisible forces in nature or appeal to divine power in order to bring out the virtues of ingredients in a remedy.

In the case of written charms, the text of the charm was occasionally passed from one sufferer to another rather like a chain-letter, although they were usually given with the injunction that they must never be opened or read.

Charms were often scriptural or sacred writings, assigned a magical value. Sometimes they were simply statements of intent. Although they were at times inscribed on amulets, often they were simply spoken.

CHAPTER 10

PLANETARY AMULETS

When making a planetary amulet, you need to be aware of the nature of each of the planets as they all rule different objects and activities.

It is best to only use materials sympathetic to that planet. On the whole, a planetary talisman has two sides and is made in a circle. One side features the magic square of the planet, while the other side shows the various sigils and signs of the planet.

Ideally, a planetary amulet is made in metal. However, you can also make it from a circle of card. The color of the cardboard should be the color of the planet, or you could use white cardboard and draw on it with ink in the planet's color. The amulet should be made on the day corresponding to the planet.

On one side of your card, draw a circle. Inside the circle, draw a square. The corners of the square may touch the periphery of the circle. Divide it up into the correct amount of squares and add the magic square numbers corresponding to the planet. Add the planet's glyph, its highest number (the sum of all the numbers in its magic square), and the name of its intelligence. On the other side of the card, draw the planet's astrological glyph, its sigil, and the sigil of its intelligence. For ease of reference, the information you will need is given below, along with the uses that can be made of each of the planetary amulets.

Planetary amulets can be made for a variety of functions. One can be made for every day of the week so that the wearer is aligned with the vibrations of the planet ruling each day. Or an amulet can be designed for a specific purpose. For example, if you wanted business success, you would make a Mercury amulet to carry around. It's traditionally recommended that you burn the wood associated with the planet while constructing it.

Planet	Glyph	Uses	Sigil	Intelligence	Number	Wood
Saturn	♄	Agriculture, construction, solidity. Protects against evil influences, helps in concentration, and gives endurance, security, power, and steadfastness. Helpful to older persons, especially in their dealings with authorities. Said to protect against death through apoplexy, cancer, decaying of the bones, consumption, dropsy, paralysis, and phthisis. Believed to protect against the danger of being buried alive while in a state of coma and the danger of violent death through secret plotting, poison or ambush. Saturn protects women during, and immediately after, childbirth. It is said that if in time of war the leader of an army hides	Agiel		45	Oak

Planet	Glyph	Uses	Sigil	Intelligence	Number	Wood
		the talisman of Saturn in a place that is in danger of falling into the enemy's hands, the enemy will be unable to cross the limits and will retreat.				
Jupiter	♃	Good fortune, prosperity, justice, authority, ambition, morals, riches, honor, and glory. It also helps you become influential and ensures that your opinions gain weight and that they are appreciated. Jupiter helps secure peace. It is related to religious things, law and order, and it makes you conscientious. It is helpful in situations that involve government agencies and law and can provide help		Yophiel	130	Pine

Planet	Glyph	Uses	Sigil	Intelligence	Number	Wood
		from superiors. Jupiter brings good will and sympathy, drives away cares, is favorable to honest enterprises, and increases well-being. It gives protection against unforeseen accidents. It is said to provide protection from death caused by diseases of the liver, inflammation of the lungs or malignant tumors.				
Mars	♂	Courage, fortitude, strength, victory, reckless deeds, violence. Mars strengthens courage and readiness to action. It brings victory in combat, fights, and arguments. Mars gives power over adversaries, and provides		Graphiel	325	Cedar

Planet	Glyph	Uses	Sigil	Intelligence	Number	Wood
		success in litigation. It offers protection against attacks from dangerous enemies. Mars is said to protect against malignant ulcers or epidemic.				
Sun	☉	Healing, wealth, friendship, nobility, authority, riches, honor, and freedom. The Sun gives good reputation, influence, power, and popularity. It helps generally in making wishes come true and provides good circumstances and a long life. The Sun brings good will and the favor of those in high positions. It is said to protect against heart disease, aneurysm, and epidemic.		Nakiel	666	Laurel

Planet	Glyph	Uses	Sigil	Intelligence	Number	Wood
Venus	♀	Love, friendship, travel, art, music, beauty, riches. Venus makes people attractive, especially to the other sex, and it causes love. It is one of the ideal amulets for love. Venus is favorable to actors, dancers, artists, jewelers, and to persons who are involved in arts and crafts. Venus preserves harmony and affection between man and wife and keeps away those who may offend by envy and hate. It is said to preserve women from cancer and protects men and women from violent death by poisoning, deliberate or accidental.		Hagiel	1225	Myrtle

Planet	Glyph	Uses	Sigil	Intelligence	Number	Wood
Mercury	☿	Communication, business, memory, eloquence, learning, intellect, science, and writing skills. Mercury activates the mind. It is good for speech, writing, authoring, studies, and travel. It is especially favorable to salesmen, travelers, journalists, and authors. Mercury is the protector of all kinds of commerce and industry. If it is buried underneath a shop or place of business, it attracts clients and prosperity. It is said to protect against attacks of epilepsy or madness and death by murder or poison. It guards against treason. If placed		Tiriel	2080	Hazel

Planet	Glyph	Uses	Sigil	Intelligence	Number	Wood
		beneath the head during sleep, it produces prophetic dreams.				
Moon	☽	Travel, success, health, dreams, religion, secrets, and women's problems. The Moon protects against dangers from water. It also protects against attacks during the night. The Moon favors all persons subject to continuous change. It protects travelers and persons dwelling in a foreign land. It is said to protect against death by shipwreck, or from epilepsy, dropsy, apoplexy, and madness.		Malcah Be-Tarshsim We-ad Ruachoth ha-chechalim	3321	Willow

CHAPTER 11

HOW TO CHOOSE THE RIGHT TIME FOR MAKING YOUR AMULET

You can make an amulet at any time. However, the more things that you consider in connection with the specific energy you want associated with your amulet, the more the amulet will contain the vibrations of that energy and it's likely to be far more effective. There are a number of ways in which you can take advantage of the time that you make your amulet. This chapter describes the most commonly used and the most straightforward.

The first stage is to be clear about the purpose of your amulet. Sometimes this can be very simple. You might want an amulet to bring more love into your life, for example. At other times, more thought might be required. You might have decided to make a protection amulet. But what do you feel you need protection from and why? Do you want to bring something into your life or remove it? It's worth spending a little time to make sure that you're clear about what you want to achieve if you haven't already done so. Make sure that you have everything you need in advance of making the amulet, and allow time for designing it.

There may be practical considerations as well. Although a Friday is generally best for making a love amulet, there could be reasons why Fridays are particularly difficult for you. In that case, you'd want to look at finding the best times on the days that are possible for you.

There are optimum times of the month, days of the week and times of day that are good moments to prepare specific types of amulets. It may not be possible for you to adhere to all of these. Don't worry if you can't. Although your amulet can be strengthened by choosing the right time, the reverse isn't true. Your amulet won't be damaged by choosing an inappropriate time – the worst that can happen is that it isn't as effective as it could be.

Choosing the Right Time of the Month – Working with the Moon

There are basically two major Moon phases – waxing and waning. The waxing Moon is increasing in size from new to full, whereas the waning Moon is decreasing in size from full to new. The Moon's cycle lasts twenty-eight days, because that's how long it takes to orbit the earth. The Moon has no natural light; the light we see is reflected from the sun. As the Moon orbits the earth, shadows are created over parts of the Moon. As a result there is only one day in this cycle that the full face of the Moon reflects the Sun's light – at full Moon. And there is only one day of the month when the Moon cannot be seen – the new Moon. This is the basis of the Moon phases.

It is quite easy to work out which phase the Moon is in. The new Moon appears to be totally dark or it may seem that there is no Moon at all. A waxing crescent is a light colored crescent on the right side of the Moon. The first quarter can be seen as the right half of the Moon is lit. The waxing gibbous Moon is when three quarters of the light of the Moon can be seen and this brings us to the full Moon.

The waning crescent from the full Moon can be seen as a dark crescent appearing on the right side of the Moon. The third quarter is when the right half of the Moon is dark. The waning gibbous Moon is three quarters dark and that brings us to the new Moon.

If you look outside at the Moon, over a few consecutive nights, you will see how this pattern occurs.

When you want to create an amulet that offers growth, or improvement, it's best to do it when the Moon is waxing or increasing from new to full. For example, an amulet to increase your wealth should certainly be done under a waxing Moon. For most amulets, a waxing Moon is best.

On the other hand, if you want to make an amulet that involves destruction or removal of some sort, then it's best to do it when the Moon is waning, or decreasing in size from full to new.

The full Moon is associated with completeness and endings. It is a good time to create amulets for protection. If you are creating an amulet to bring extra power, such as help finding a new job or healing for serious conditions, this can be a good time. The full Moon is also often used for love, knowledge, legal undertakings, and money amulets.

The new Moon is best for new ventures. It is particularly good for love and romance, and job hunting.

Moon in the Zodiac Signs

If you are able to find out what sign the Moon is in, this information can also be used to increase the success of your amulet. You can buy books of tables or almanacs to find out the Moon's sign on a particular date, or you can look it up on the Internet. The Moon stays about two and a half days in each sign.

Moon in Aries – Good for amulets related to authority and willpower. A positive time to for starting things, but can lack staying power. Things happen but quickly pass.

Moon in Taurus – Good for amulets related to your personal finances and possessions. Things begun now last the longest, tend to increase in value, and become harder to alter.

Moon in Gemini – Good for amulets related to relatives, communication, studies, and writing. Things begun now are easily changed by outside influences.

Moon in Cancer – Good for amulets related to domestic matters, your home, and family. Supports growth and nurturance.

Moon in Leo – Good for amulets related to pleasures, hobbies, love affairs, children, entertainment, sports, and your pets. Can add a sense of drama.

Moon in Virgo – Good for amulets related to your day-to-day work and routine matters and health. Favors accomplishment of details.

Moon in Libra – Good for amulets related to love and partnerships or legal matters. Increases self awareness and interaction with others.

Moon in Scorpio – Good for amulets related to debts, inheritance, and secrets. Can end connections

Moon in Sagittarius – Good for amulets related to long-distance travel, in-laws, truth, and higher learning. Encourages flights of imagination and confidence.

Moon in Capricorn – Good for amulets related to business, politics, career, and reputation. Increases awareness of the need for structure and discipline.

Moon in Aquarius – Good for amulets related to friendship, acquaintances, hopes and dreams, groups and organizations. Favors activities that are unique and individualistic.

Moon in Pisces – Good for amulets related to music, creativity, inner development and revealing secrets. Can increase psychic awareness but also lead to confusion.

The Right Day

The most straightforward way of timing when to make your amulet is to work on the day that corresponds to its purpose. A planet rules each day of the week and matters associated with those planets are best done on their own day.

Monday	=	Moon
Tuesday	=	Mars
Wednesday	=	Mercury
Thursday	=	Jupiter
Friday	=	Venus
Saturday	=	Saturn
Sunday	=	Sun

Monday

Monday is ruled by the Moon. This means that amulets created for purposes associated with the Moon are best created on this day.

Amulets – those to do with emotional matters; intuition; women's issues; motherhood; the sea; the home and domestic matters; short trips; pregnancy; fertility; and childbirth.

According to tradition three specific Mondays in the year are considered to be unlucky – the first Monday in April, the second in August, and the last in December. It is said that Cain was born on the first Monday in April, and that later it was upon this day that he killed his brother Abel. Sodom and Gomorrah was said to be destroyed on the second Monday in August, and that it was upon the last Monday in December that Judas Iscariot was born.

Tuesday

Named for the Norse god Tiw, Tuesday is ruled by his Roman counterpart, Mars.

Amulets – those to do with quarrels; drugs; courage; boldness; power; war; male issues; lust; energy; willpower; discord; surgery; and sex.

It's traditionally unlucky to meet a left-handed person on a Tuesday morning. This is because Tiw was left-handed and sacrificed his right hand to the wolf for the good of his people.

Wednesday

This day was associated with Woden, or Odin, the god of war, wisdom, agriculture, and poetry. He was also regarded as the god of the Dead. Wednesday is associated with the planet Mercury, and in French its name is *Mercredi* or "Mercury's Day." Mercury is the god of science, commerce, travellers, rogues, and thieves.

Amulets – those to do with wit; intelligence; communication; news; speech; education, employment; exams; short distance travel; trade and business; contracts; letters; and cars.

In most of Europe, Wednesday was thought to be a very unlucky day, whilst in the USA quite the opposite was believed. The Persians associated Wednesday with the name "Red Letter Day." It is said that this was because they believed that the Moon was created on Wednesday.

Thursday

Thursday was originally associated with two gods, Jove and Thor. Thor was the god of thunder hence the day also being known a "thunder day." Jove – or Jupiter – was also known to be associated with thunder, with the French renaming the day *Jeudi* which means "Jove's Day."

Amulets – those to do with good luck in general; happiness; fidelity; career; reputation; religion; law; gambling; speculation; higher education; and wealth.

In Germany, Thursday was believed traditionally to be the unluckiest day of the week. As a result, the practice grew of ensuring that no important business should be carried out, no marriages held and even that no child should be sent to school for their first time on this day. The hour before sunrise is traditionally considered lucky, even though it's ruled by Saturn.

Friday

The name given to Friday in ancient Rome was *dies Veneris* as is was a day dedicated to Venus. Later the French named the day *Vendredi*, believed to have derived from the same origin. In northern countries, the closest equivalent to the Goddess Venus was Frigg or Freya, with the day becoming known by the Anglo-Saxons as "Frige dag," later changing to Friday.

Amulets – those to do with affection; love; enjoyment; amusement; music, beauty; friendship; clothes; women; wives; mothers; social life; gifts; money; and marriage.

Friday is traditionally associated in many parts of Europe with misfortune, as this was believed to be the day when Christ was crucified and also the day that Adam was tempted by Eve with the forbidden fruit. According to tradition there are some practices that should be avoided on a Friday including, births, weddings, the sailing of a ship, cutting your nails or starting a new job. In the past, Friday was the customary day to carry out hangings and so was sometimes referred to as "Hangman's Day" or "Hanging Day." However, Friday has always been thought of as a good day as far as romance is concerned.

Saturday

The Latin name for this day was *Dies Saturni* meaning the "Day of Saturn." Saturn was associated with the ancient Greek Kronos or Time.

Amulets – those for responsibility; ambition; self discipline; restrictions; and obligations. In general, not a good day for making amulets.

Saturday has been considered to be the most unlucky day of the week in most cultures. In India, it's traditionally believed to be unlucky as it's the day dedicated to the god of misfortune, named Sani – people in India never marry on a Saturday. It was traditionally believed to be bad luck to change jobs on a Saturday.

Sunday

The origin of the word Sunday is rooted in the Germanic *Sonntag*. Sunday celebrates the Sun Gods, Ra, Helios, Sol, Apollo, and Mithras. In 321AD, the Emperor Constantine ruled that the first day of the week – the day of the Sun – should be a day of rest.

Amulets – those for power; authority and obtaining a favor; friendship; prosperity; and status.

Sunday is a good day traditionally for healing illnesses. Any cures that are administered on a Sunday were believed to be more likely to succeed.

Planetary Hours

Finally, if you want to be really specific, you can choose the best hour of the day for making your amulet. In the same way as you can choose the right day according to its association with a suitable planet, you can find a time of day ruled by the planet that is most closely connected with your amulet. Unfortunately, this isn't quite so simple as just looking at a clock.

Instead of assuming the day starts when the date changes, at midnight, planetary hours are based on a one-twelfth division of the hours between sunrise and sunset. This means that the length of the hours will vary according to the time of year.

At the Spring equinox (around 21 March) and the autumn equinox (around 21 September), day and night are approximately the same length. At this time, a planetary hour is almost the same as a clock hour. In midsummer (around 21 June), daytime is much longer than night. There can be eighteen hours of daylight in some places. The winter solstice (around 21 December) has the shortest day, sometimes as low as six hours.

This means that a planetary hour in late December will only be a half hour of clock time, whereas a planetary hour in late June can be as long as two hours. This is how the hours of the day were calculated in the distant past before the more convenient, equal-length hours were introduced.

The planetary hour after sunrise on each day is ruled by the planet that rules that day. For example, the hour after sunrise on any Monday is ruled by the Moon. The following hours are then ruled by the planets in this sequence – Moon, Saturn, Jupiter, Mars, Sun, Venus, Mercury. When you reach the end of the sequence, you simply begin again.

To be able to calculate planetary hours for any day, you need to know the times of sunrise and sunset for your location. You can often find these in diaries, almanacs, tide tables, local newspapers (in the weather section) and on the Internet.

The calculations are quite straightforward, although you might find it useful to have a calculator to hand. Let's suppose that we're calculating the planetary hours for a Sunday when sunrise is at 5 am and sunset at 7 pm.

The first thing to note is that there are fourteen hours of day. We'll assume that you want to calculate your amulet during the daytime, but if for some reason you'd like to do it at night, the method is the same.

Next, we multiply 14 by 60 – the number of minutes in an hour. This is simply to make calculations easier, as often the times of sunrise and sunset won't be exactly on the hour. In this example, our answer is 840 minutes.

We divide 840 by 12 to find out the length of each planetary hour. The answer is seventy minutes, or one hour and ten minutes.

As this is a Sunday, the first planetary hour after sunrise is ruled by the Sun. Sunrise is at 5 am. Adding one hour and ten minutes brings us to 6:10 am, which is the end of the Sun hour.

The hour after the Sun hour is the Venus hour. This starts at 6:10 am and if we add one hour and ten minutes, this brings us to 7:20 am, which will be the start of the Mercury hour. The Moon hour begins at 8:30 am, Saturn hour at 9:40 am, Jupiter hour at 10:50 am, Mars hour at 12 noon, and then we return to the Sun hour at 1:10 pm. The second Venus hour of the day begins at 2:20 pm, Mercury hour at 3:30 pm, Moon hour at 4:40 pm, Saturn hour at 5: 50 pm and this ends at sunset at 7 pm.

If we were calculating the planetary hours at night, we would begin with noting that there are 10 hours between 7 pm and 5 am. This is equivalent to 600 minutes, which divided by twelve is 50 minutes. Therefore, we would add fifty minutes to the end of each planetary hour. Sunset was at 7 pm, and as this was then the end of the Saturn hour, this brings us to the beginning of the Jupiter hour. The sequence is continued until we reach sunrise on Monday. And if your calculations are correct, you'll find that this will be a Moon hour!

If you wanted to make an amulet to attract love to you on this Sunday, you'd choose a Venus hour. This gives you the choice on this date of the times between 6:10 am to 7:20 am – and the far more civilized time of 2:20 to 3:30 pm!

Planetary hours are useful when you can't wait until the right day. For instance, if you were making a money amulet, you'd want to do it on a Thursday. Ideally, you'd do it during the Jupiter hour on a Thursday. However, if for some reason that wasn't possible, you could at least choose the Jupiter hour on the day that you have chosen.

END PIECE

Hopefully, you haven't even waited until you've reached the end of the book, but have already begun to make your own amulets. There is a lot of information contained here, but there's never any need to use it all at once. The best amulets are those with a clear purpose that are simply made. Choose the methods and materials that best suit your needs, or experiment until you find a way of working you're comfortable with. Amulets can be highly personal, and there isn't an absolute right or wrong way of going about making them. If you decide on an approach that is different to those contained in this book, that's fine. There should be enough information here to enable you to make your own decisions and come up with your own ideas.

Be lucky!

O books
O is a symbol of the world, of oneness and unity. In certain cultures it also means the "eye", symbolising knowledge and insight, and in Old English it means "place of love or home". O Books explore the many paths of wholeness and understanding which different traditions have developed through the ages.

BOOKS

In philosophy, metaphysics and aesthetics O represents zero relating to immensity, indivisibility and fate. This list challenges systems and assumptions where "nothing" is absent but substance is still missing.

For more information on the full list of over 300 titles please visit our website **www.O-books.net**

myspiritradio is an exciting web, internet, podcast and mobile phone global broadcast network for all those interested in teaching and learning in the fields of body, mind, spirit and self development. Listeners can hear the show online via computer or mobile phone, and even download their favourite shows to listen to on MP3 players whilst driving, working, or relaxing.

mySpiritRadio

Feed your mind, change your life with O Books,
The O Books radio programme carries interviews with most authors, sharing their wisdom on life, the universe and everything...e mail questions and co-create the show with O Books and myspiritradio.

Just visit **www.myspiritradio.com** for more information.

The 9 Dimensions of the Soul
Essence and the Enneagram
David Hey

The first book to relate the two, understanding the personality types of the Enneagram in relation to the Essence, shedding a new light on our personality, its origins and how it operates. Written in a beautifully simple, insightful and heartful way and transmits complex material in a way that is easy to read and understand. **Thomas O. Trobe**, Founder and Director of Learning Love Seminars, Inc.
1846940028 176pp **£10.99 $19.95**

Aim for the Stars...Reach the Moon
How to coach your life to spiritual and material success
Conor Patterson

A fascinating, intelligent, and beneficial tool and method of programming your mind for success. The techniques are fast to achieve, motivating, and inspiring. I highly recommend this book. **Uri Geller**
1905047274 208pp **£11.99 $19.95**

Developing Spiritual Intelligence
The power of you
Altazar Rossiter

This beautifully clear and fascinating book is an incredibly simple guide to that which so many of us search for. **Dr Dina Glouberman**
1905047649 240pp **£12.99 $19.95**

Don't Get MAD Get Wise
Why no one ever makes you angry, ever!
Mike George

There is a journey we all need to make, from anger, to peace, to forgiveness. Anger always destroys, peace always restores, and forgiveness always heals. This explains the journey, the steps you can take to make it happen for you.

1905047827 160pp **£7.99 $14.95**

Happiness in 10 Minutes
Brian Mountford

Brian Mountford-in exploring "happiness"-celebrates the paradox of losing and finding at its heart. At once both profound and simple, the book teaches us that to be fully alive is to be in communion and that gratitude leads us into the mystery of giving ourselves away-the path of true joy.
Alan Jones, Dean of Grace Cathedral, San Francisco, author of *Reimagining Christianity.*

1905047770 112pp b/w illustrations **£6.99 $9.95**

Head Versus Heart-and our Gut Reactions
The 21st century enneagram
Michael Hampson

A seminal work, whose impact will continue to reverberate throughout the 21st century. Brings illumination and allows insights to tumble out.
Fr Alexander, Worth Abbey

19038169000 320pp **£11.99 $16.95**

Love, Healing and Happiness
Spiritual wisdom for a post-secular era
Larry Culliford

This will become a classic book on spirituality. It is immensely practical and grounded. It mirrors the author's compassion and lays the foundation for a higher understanding of human suffering and hope. **Reinhard Kowalski** Consultant Clinical Psychologist
1905047916 304pp **£10.99 $19.95**

The Quest
Exploring a sense of soul
Dawes, Dolley and Isaksen

This remarkable course draws on a wide variety of psychospiritual approaches. Not another hyped up DIY book but rather a carefully considered and comprehensive guide. Invaluable. **Scientific and Medical Network Review**
1903816939 264pp **£9.99 $16.95**

Zen Economics
Save the world and yourself by saving
Robert van de Weyer

This book carries several messages of hope, which are linked by the theme of saving and investing. Its single most important message is that in the western world most of us have reached a point of prosperity where the investment with the highest rate of return is investing in the self.
1903816785 96pp **£6.99 $14.95**